Learning to tell

a handbook for inclusive storytelling

Nicola Grove

British Library Cataloguing in Publication Data

A CIP record for this book is available from the Public Library

© BILD Publications 2009

BILD Publications is the imprint of:
British Institute of Learning Disabilities
Campion House
Green Street
Kidderminster
Worcestershire
DY10 1JL

Telephone: 01562 723010
Fax: 01562 723029
E-mail: enquiries@bild.org.uk
Website: www.bild.org.uk

No part of this publication may be reproduced without prior permission from the publishers, except for the quotation of brief passages for review, teaching or reference purposes, when an acknowledgement of the source must be given.

ISBN: 978 1 905218 09 7

Printed in the UK by Latimer Trend & Company Ltd, Plymouth

Illustrations by: Robin Meader

BILD Publications are distributed by:

Book Source
50 Cambuslang Road
Cambuslang
Glasgow
G32 8NB

Telephone: 0845 370 0067
Fax: 0845 370 0064

For a publications catalogue with details of all BILD books and journals telephone 01562 723010, e-mail: enquiries@bild.org.uk or visit the BILD website: www.bild.org.uk

Acknowledgements

We are grateful to the following people for their help in contributing ideas:

- Fiona Green from the Openstorytellers for the 'Name dice' game.

- Stopgap dance company for the 'Pass the touch' game.

- The Devil's Violin and Daniel Morden for the 'Come to see the king' game.

- Nancy Mellon for the Indian ritual dance.

- Jem Dick for the 'Into the middle' game.

- Louise Coigley, Lis'n Tell for her puppets and pictures ideas, her 'seven basic gestures' and her eye contact tips.

- Michael White for his ideas used for 'presence of the storyteller'.

- Ben Haggerty for providing the inspiration for the development of the Khavad.

- Vicki Bishop from OCN South West for her help with accreditation.

About the British Institute of Learning Disabilities

The British Institute of Learning Disabilities is committed to improving the quality of life for people with a learning disability by involving them and their families in all aspects of our work, working with the government and public bodies to achieve full citizenship, undertaking beneficial research and development projects and helping service providers to develop and share good practice.

About this book

This resource aims to develop the following skills:

- recalling, telling and responding to a range of stories with different audiences

- working in a group

- self-reflection and self-monitoring

It is primarily designed to enable students to find personal meaning in traditional stories, and so make links between a legend and their own lives. You can use these materials flexibly (or integrate them into a more formal course for accreditation).

This resource is unique in its approach to the culture of oral storytelling. Traditional stories are often told by a single, fluent narrator who is in full control of a range of stories, impressing the audience through his or her verbal skills. Our approach to storytelling emphasises the participatory and communal aspects that develop an intensity of listening to the storyteller and an atmosphere in which a contribution told from the heart is valued for what it communicates about our common humanity. With a raft of information, forms, video footage, games, activities and stories, this resource can help students develop an ability to narrate, which is fundamental to human experience.

The DVD that accompanies this book contains video footage relating to the text and PDFs of all the forms for ease of printing and/or distribution.

You may want to use these materials to deliver an accredited course for the learners.

About Openstorytellers

Openstorytellers is the new name of the Unlimited Company of Storytellers. We are now an independent charity.

Openstorytellers is a unique group of community storytellers who have learning disabilities. The group grew out of a project to develop storytelling skills, which ran from 2004–2007. The group is based in Somerset, but works all over the country and internationally. It is a social enterprise, co-run by people with and without learning disabilities.

The members of the group from 2004–2007 when this resource was developed were:

Jem Dick	Nicola Grove	Joel Reboul
Paul Dickens	Jane Harwood	Catherine Rolfe
Heather Dickinson	Isobel Herdon	Derryn Street, Somerset Community Team for Adults with Learning Disabilities
Hazel Elders	Brian Marshall	
Ann Gould	Ian Matthews	Louise Lisle, Somerset Total Communication
Trudy Graves	Robin Meader	
Barbara Green	James Norman	Steve Maris, Mencap
Fiona Green	Wendy North	

The work of the group was made possible by grants from the following organisations, which we gratefully acknowledge:

The Big Lottery Fund	The Esmée Fairbairn Foundation
The Arts Council	Somerset County Council

We are also grateful to BILD for their management of our project and to the Community Team for Adults with Learning Disabilities in Mendip for their secondment of a member of staff and help with accommodation and administration.

And to members of our steering group:

Jane Jones, BILD

Nicola Epps, Arts Development Officer, Somerset

Caroline Conlon, Somerset Community Team for Adults with Learning Disabilities

Sue Eadie, Somerset Community Team for Adults with Learning Disabilities

Neil Galloway, Head Teacher, Avalon School

Nell Farrelly, Merlin Theatre

Karin Purvis, Head of Speech and Language Therapy Service, Somerset Partnership and Social Care Trust

Sue Jennings, independent consultant and storyteller

Rosemary Westlake, Carer representative

Openstorytellers, c/o Black Swan Arts, 2 Bridge Street, Frome, BA11 1BB
www.openstorytellers.org.uk

Learning to tell

Contents of the Book

Section 9:
Appendices

Learning to tell

Contents of the DVD

Extract 1:   The Unlimited Company introduce themselves
Extract 2:   Story theme: Loss, disability, rebirth –
               Performance of Ceridwen's Cauldron
Extract 3:   Story theme: Discussion
Extract 4:   Story lines 1: Life story
Extract 5:   Story lines 2: Personal photos
Extract 6:   Story lines 3: Personal anecdote
Extract 7:   Story lines 4: Portfolio examples
Extract 8:   Story skills: Structural 1 – Memory game
Extract 9:   Story skills: Structural 2 – Story components
Extract 10:   Story skills: Structural 3 – Characters
Extract 11:   Story skills: Structural 4 – Sequencing
Extract 12:   Story skills: Structural 5 – Storytelling with the Khavad
Extract 13:   Story skills: Feelings 1 – Facial expressions
Extract 14:   Story skills: Feelings 2 – Gestures
Extract 15:   Story skills: Feelings 3 – Voice
Extract 16:   Story skills: Feelings 4 – Voice and gesture
Extract 17:   Story skills: Feelings 5 – Putting it together
Extract 18:   Story skills: Language description
Extract 19:   Story skills: Social 1 – Bad telling
Extract 20:   Story skills: Social 2 – Good telling
Extract 21:   Story skills: Social 3 – Bad listening
Extract 22:   Story skills: Social 4 – Good listening
Extract 23:   Story company 1   Physical warm-ups
Extract 24:   Story company 2   Voice warm-ups
Extract 25:   Story company 3   Opening games – Minestrone
Extract 26:   Story company 4   Opening games – Pass the clap
Extract 27:   Story company 5   Opening games – Pass the touch
Extract 28:   Story company 6   News introduction
Extract 29:   Story company 7   News small group
Extract 30:   Story company 8   News feedback
Extract 31:   Story company 9   Group support strategies
Extract 32:   Story company 10   Group problem solving
Extract 33:   Story company 11   Group rules
Extract 34:   Story company 12   Shared memories at lunchtime
Extract 35:   Story company 13   Symbolic ritual
Extract 36:   Story company 14   Feedback circle
Extract 37:   Story company 15   Closing game
Extract 38:   I am a storyteller

Learning to tell

Section 1:
About storytelling

1.1   The importance of storytelling

The ability to narrate is fundamental to human experience. Human beings have always told each other stories, whether great myths and legends or just the events of everyday life.

Nowadays, storytelling is increasingly gaining recognition as an art form that sustains and expresses cultural identity. There are many opportunities for people who wish to develop their skills as storytellers – at festivals, on courses and in story circles. But, if you have difficulties with language and communication, these opportunities are not very accessible. Oral storytelling has always been a very demanding skill, requiring a good memory, a high level of linguistic competence, flexibility in perceiving and adapting to the audience, imagination and dramatic flair, and great self-confidence. This book is designed to support inclusive storytelling, and reflects our emphasis on participation by people who may have a range of learning disabilities or special educational needs.

1.2   Ethos

The philosophy underpinning this book is that everyone has stories that are worth telling, and deserve to be heard and valued. People have different skills and styles, and tell stories in different ways using gestures, facial expressions, pictures, signs and symbols as well as their voices.

Our model of storytelling is a social model, that is, stories (and the skills needed to tell them) are learned through participating directly in the act of storytelling. The role of the trainer is to develop and build the abilities of everyone in the group; provide a rich source of stories to draw on; and show by example how stories can be told together.

This book is unique in its approach to the culture of oral storytelling. Traditional stories are often told by a single, fluent narrator who is in full control of a range of stories, impressing the audience through his or her verbal skills. Our approach to storytelling emphasises the participatory and communal aspects that develop an intensity of listening to the storyteller and an atmosphere in which a contribution told from the heart is valued for what it communicates about our common humanity. We seek to make connections between powerful archetypal traditional myths and the lived experience of day-to-day challenges and triumphs, and to illuminate the importance of the small, the unnoticed and the unorthodox for our audiences.

1.3 Why is storytelling important for people with learning disabilities?

The role of stories in the lives of people with learning disabilities is just the same as for everyone else – stories are fun and interesting, help you to make friends, understand the world and develop your imagination. When you remember things that have happened to you, you can share the good things (and the bad) through telling others, who then help you to feel proud of yourself, or cope with a bad experience. Traditional legends offer us hopes, dreams and possibilities, as one storyteller, Robin, makes clear when talking about Aladdin:

> 'What I like about it is that it's a really good story about how he started out as a poor washing boy, and it reminded me of when I was young. I was always a little boy and could do nothing but play with toys, watch TV and read books, but like Aladdin I always had to do a lot of washing. But one day Aladdin discovered he wanted to go somewhere he could find a magic lamp, and it's like me when I feel like I really want to go out to a place to visit, like a castle or a cave or something. And as he rubs the lamp a genie comes out with the three wishes and it reminds me of wanting to get a job and make a lot of money. And then he falls in love with this girl and becomes rich, and to me it makes me feel like I want to go out in the world and talk to people.'

Recent developments in the fields of self-advocacy and person-centred planning have highlighted the role of narrative and story in the development of a strong and coherent sense of identity. Storytelling is a crucial life skill. We need to construct a narrative every time we describe a problem – to the doctor, to the police or to the council, etc. Moreover, in learning to make independent decisions, the ability to recall and reflect on the meaning of our experiences is also critical. We can only make informed choices if we can remember the consequences of a previous similar decision, and our reactions to it. Thus, storytelling is a functional skill that supports personal development, as well as opening the door to rich imaginative worlds and enabling people to become familiar with their own cultural heritage.

1.4 **Our framework and teaching**

There are many different approaches to the teaching of storytelling, and all of them involve slightly different definitions of what a story and/or a storyteller is. For example, in one framework that is extensively taught in schools, a story is defined as centring on a hero who solves a problem that is usually told by one person as a monologue. This is fine for traditional legends, and indeed is usually what you will encounter at story festivals and story circles. But it does not work so well for anecdotal storytelling, where often groups of friends or families all tell a story together, and where the story is not necessarily built around a problem, but around an event which is a departure from routine, and therefore interesting and 'reportable'. We have found that collaborative telling about reportable events is the best place to start for people who have communication difficulties and who are nervous of storytelling. **(See extracts 6 and 34 on the accompanying DVD).**

Our framework for stories involves:

- **Who** – the people

- **When** and/or **where** – the setting

- **What happened** – the main events

- **The sparkle** – the unexpected, interesting climax

- **How you felt** – the emotions associated with the events that you want the audience to feel as well

- **What was said** – the reactions and exclamations of the people in the story

1.5 **Our storytellers**

As Brian Marshall (another of our storytellers) memorably stated at the end of a public performance of an Arthurian legend linked to his own experience,

> 'We all have stories, don't we?'

But we often need help and support to tell them. So, when we look at our storytellers, we are looking for any way that they can convey the different aspects of the story. That is the role of the teacher/trainer and story partner. Some people will not be so good at talking, but good at gesture – so we build on that. Others can convey the atmosphere and the feelings of the story through body language or imaginative use of musical instruments or props. Our stories are not told through speech alone, but through total communication (usually defined as all the resources available for understanding and expression: auditory–vocal; visual–gestural–movement; use of objects; use of smell, taste and touch). Gradually, as people practise their stories with support, they will memorise them, develop a wider range of resources and become more autonomous storytellers.

Section 2:
Principles for inclusive storytelling

2.1 The four strands of storytelling

The content of this book integrates four strands of storytelling. These strands are:

- **Story themes**
- **Story lines**
- **Story skills**
- **Story company**

Story themes

The function of the story themes is to nourish the imagination of the group with powerful and resonant symbols and to develop personal myth making. They are developed through the telling of stories at the beginning and end of the day, and by work done on the meaning of these stories. By taking a theme, stories can be chosen systematically, and can be linked rather than just selected at random as good stories.

Story lines

The story lines strand involves the collection and development of different kinds of story, which are recorded in personal portfolios and chosen by the students themselves.

Story skills

The story skills strand involves exercises and games to practise specific strategies for telling and listening.

Story company

The story company strand involves the development of a sense of group identity and social skills.

2.2 **Story themes**

To effectively deliver inclusive storytelling it is best to select a theme for a week, term or period of work that relates to the fundamentals of storytelling:

- What is a story?
- Where do stories originate?
- Who are the storytellers?
- Who owns the story?
- What does it mean?
- What do stories do for us?

A group calendar can be used to plan appropriate story themes. The DVD that accompanies this book shows one example of a story theme 'Ceridwen's Cauldron'. The key themes are identified as disability, loss and rebirth. **(See extracts 2 and 3 on the accompanying DVD).**

What stories are told?

Within this resource, story themes are developed through the telling of traditional stories. These include:

- **Myths** – sacred stories communicating the beliefs of particular cultures: stories of the gods and the heavens.

- **Legends and hero tales** – stories about people who live or might have lived a long time ago and whose deeds were so marvellous that we remember them and are inspired by them.

- **Wonder tales** – tales of magic and imagination; of other worlds that exist alongside our own; fairy tales.

- **Folk and fable** – tales of ordinary people doing ordinary things from which we can learn. Often these are told about animals as though they were human.

When we tell these stories, we identify them for our audience with symbols or pictures (such as the illustrations you see here), gestures, and with a consistent introduction, eg '*This is a myth – it's a story about creation.*'

Context for telling

Story themes can be experienced in the large group, and then discussed in small groups, where links can be made between the story and personal responses and experience. (See extract 2 on the accompanying DVD).

Activities

Activities in story theme work involve the telling of the stories and discussion of topics and genres, eg ghost stories, funny stories, romance. The large group focus of the story theme emphasises performance storytelling, and storytelling community and culture.

Learning opportunities

Experiences during story theme work enable students to:

- build up their knowledge of traditional stories

- understand the connections between their own lives and a traditional story

- develop their skills in storytelling performance

- learn how to act as a responsive audience

Themes

This book identifies a range of themes:

- time and the seasons

- place (eg local folklore)

- company/group dynamics

- disability and personal experiences

Time and the seasons

Seasonal themes are important to include because of the connection with the cycle of time and the natural order, which underpins and gives meaning to stories.

At the individual level, the seasons often mark out the experiences we remember: holidays, Christmas presents, Easter eggs and birthdays. At the level of the local community, knowledge of seasonal stories helps us to choose what to tell. As we are based in Somerset, where Celtic history is very important, we used the Celtic calendar and associated legends:

- *Samhain (pronounced sow-ain)* 31 October
- *Imbolc (im-bolk)* 31 January
- *Beltane (bel-tane)* 1 May
- *Lughnasadh (loo-na-sah)* 31 July

Figure 1 (on page 25) shows an example calendar or cycle of story themes.

You can use your own selection of myths and legends, and can refer to a calendar of cultural and religious festivals to help you plan.

Figure 1 **Example cycle of story themes in a one-year inclusive storytelling programme**

Term	Time	Place	Personal	Company dynamics	Disability
Autumn	Harvest Samhain/ Hallowe'en Jewish New Year Guy Fawkes Diwali Chanukah Eid Christmas *Focus in year one is on familiar well-known stories*		Will form part of personal portfolios, constructed to make links between the personal SMALL and the traditional BIG story Birthdays and holidays and personal special dates	Beginnings – *creation stories* Coming together, forming identity 'Just so'-type stories about characteristic behaviours How stories are made Origins and role of stories in our lives	Be aware of personal stories about experiences of disability, with images of disability Make a note of any representations of people with disabilities that feature in our stories
Spring	New Year Chinese New Year Imbolg St Valentine Passover Easter			Bonding as a group – Arthur's knights The end of the Round Table	Sir Gareth Sir Perceval and Sir Galahad Sir Gawain and the Loathly Lady
Summer	Beltane/May Day Whitsun Lammas	West Country local folktales		Achievement Flowering Farewell The breaking of the Round Table: King Arthur's successors	

Place

Site-specific stories are important when planning and delivering storytelling events, and choosing which stories to tell. For example, the 300th anniversary of the granting of the town charter to Glastonbury fell during our own inclusive storytelling programme. This meant that we chose to tell some Arthurian legends, which also linked to group identity. Local folklore helps us to understand more about our communities. At the individual level, specific places are often important in personal histories.

Company dynamics

Our story themes for the first year reflected the focus of the group: coming together as individuals in a new situation; bonding as a team, planning and plotting, ideas and inspiration; achievement, flowering and harvest; and endings and looking forward to new beginnings. The work of Alida Gersie in planning story themes was very helpful. Her books are listed in Section 8. Threaded into these themes were stories associated with the cycle of the year and seasonal festivals.

When selecting stories, your choices may need to reflect and support the management of the group dynamics. You may also need to be flexible and alert to the personal experiences of individuals – for example if there is a loss, bereavement or accident, or a celebration that affects a group member, you may decide to tell a story which reflects this.

Disability

At the beginning of our project, we assumed that disability and its representation would be central to the identity of the developing company. Many of our group were involved in the local advocacy movement. However, rather than imposing this, we waited to see how this theme emerged through the stories that people told themselves.

We always took opportunities to address issues of discrimination, bullying and physical appearance as they arose within stories. For example, the tale of Sir Gareth, which we told as part of an Arthurian cycle linked to the Glastonbury celebrations, features the bullying of Gareth by Sir Kay on account of his lowly status. This had very obvious relevance to some of our group who had experienced discrimination at work and name calling. Other Arthurian legends are useful here: Sir Galahad and Sir Perceval are both types of 'holy fool', and Sir Gawain's interactions with an ugly old woman raise issues of prejudice and discrimination on the basis of age and appearance. The company began to address disability issues more directly as we moved into the second and third years of our work. It was a natural development from a more outward-looking focus, as we engaged with issues in the world, went out to conferences and ran training sessions.

2.3 Story lines: collecting and sharing personal stories

This strand involves the collection and development of different kinds of story in personal portfolios. Various examples of story lines are provided on the DVD that accompanies this book. **(See extracts 4–7 on the accompanying DVD).** Central to the story lines strand is the emphasis on the experience of telling and listening to stories, so that space is provided each week in the small groups for anyone who wishes to tell a story, ensuring that all participants build up confidence in themselves as narrators. Small groups are also given the opportunity to choose and practise a story to tell collaboratively in the large groups.

Personal narratives

This kind of story involves the collection of personal narratives that focus on significant events and/or everyday happenings. These story lines weave together to produce the fabric of our lives as remembered experiences. Personal narratives include those heard from other people. The natural context is conversational, between two or three people and small groups.

Media narratives

Media narratives are stories that resonate for us in some way and derive from the media: TV, radio, film, newspapers and magazines. They may be fictional or real – news stories, soaps and celebrity stories. Again, these stories are usually told within conversations. A brief example can be found on the DVD that accompanies this book. **(See extract 30 on the accompanying DVD.)**

Traditional stories

Traditional stories include myth, wonder tales, folk tales and legends. They are the stories used for story theme work. In the story lines context, these are the stories chosen by individuals as particularly significant to them. They may come from the stories told during inclusive storytelling sessions, or from pantomime, theatre or cinema, TV, DVD or audiotape, or through the reading of picture books. The conversational context of the small group is used to help the person tell the story informally, before progressing to telling in the large group, and to explore links between the theme story and personal stories of individuals.

Examples of questions to ask during conversational small group discussions might be:

- Have you ever felt like Sir Gareth?

- How did things change for you?

- Are there people who sometimes talk like Kay and Linet (the people who bully Gareth) in your life?

The DVD that accompanies this book offers an example of a powerful life story, which has connections with the disability theme in Ceridwen's story. **(See extract 4 on the accompanying DVD.)**

Ways of telling and recording

There are many ways to tell or record the stories.

Video story

Have a video camera set up for people to go and tell stories in a quiet place at lunchtime. Each person needs their own cassette, which should be kept somewhere accessible and safe.

Writing stories down

Stories can be written down by the group using their own words as far as possible, even if there are gaps. Group participants can also dictate the stories to the teacher/trainer to be included in the portfolios. However, in practice, dictation is only possible for very important stories because it can prove time-consuming.

Outlines

Using outlines is probably the best and quickest way of recording stories. When someone tells a story that they want to record, they draw pictures of the key events and people, using the prompts (*who, when, where, what happened, feelings*). The story is given a title, and they then have the responsibility of remembering it by telling it over and over again. An example sheet is provided in the Appendices section at the end of this book. See Appendix 1.

Portfolios

Portfolios are the cumulative records of stories collected over time. The DVD that accompanies this book offers an example of a portfolio with both personal and traditional stories. **(See extract 7 on the accompanying DVD.)**

You can start with information similar to that collected in a communication passport, which is a resource developed to collect key information about the lives of people with communication difficulties: *this is me, where I live, likes and dislikes, hopes and dreams, my family and friends.*

This can be followed by personal history – stories from childhood, family stories, triumphs and disasters, key experiences such as *leaving school, getting work experience, joining an advocacy group.*

2.4 Story skills: learning to listen and helping to tell

Story skills involve the specific skills associated with telling and listening to stories, within a participatory framework/model that emphasises the collaborative nature of storytelling.

The story skills strand involves exercises and games to practise specific strategies for telling, categorised into four aspects:

- structural
- feelings
- language
- social

This strand also includes implicit work in modelling good storytelling and poor practice, and reinforcement of what people are doing well (by noticing and commenting). Later in the inclusive storytelling programme, when people have gained confidence, they will watch themselves on film and work directly with their own strengths and needs.

Structural

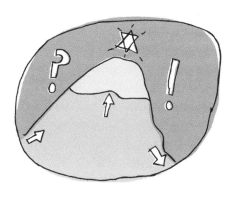

The structural games and exercises have been designed to develop the skills needed for memory and sequencing of events; the inclusion of narrative elements (like summary of events, time and place, characters, events leading to climax, high point of story, etc); an ending/resolution for the story. **(See extracts 8–11 on the accompanying DVD.)**

Feelings

These exercises and games refer to how people felt, and judgements made, about events, people and places (for example 'it was good'). They also develop the use of intonation, stress and repetition, and help participants learn how to show engagement with the story by using facial expressions and gestures. **(See extracts 13–17 on the accompanying DVD.)**

Language

These exercises and games refer to the range of language used – how rich and varied in choice of nouns, verbs, adjectives, adverbs; use of different verb tenses; and the use of complex clause structure and linking words such as *because, when, then, so, if*. Use of poetic language functioning like music to give a pattern and rhythm to the story eg repetitions (*again and again*); story language (*once upon a time*), figures of speech such as metaphors, similes and well-known phrases or sayings. **(See extract 18 on the accompanying DVD.)**

Social

These games and exercises cover awareness of the audience; introduction and closure of the story that makes reference to the audience; eye contact, feedback, incorporation of audience reactions; and response to questions, listening, co-construction, awareness of needs of others.

Story skills are explicitly assessed each term – through qualitative records kept by the trainers, and formally with video. In your planning, try to target them systematically each week in workshops. Figure 3 later in this book provides an example of a cycle of story skills, and you will find examples of games and activities for story skills in Sections 3 and 4 of this book.

2.5 **Story company**

This strand involves the development of a sense of group identity, through games, the discussion of group rules and conventions, and the use of particular rituals, such as: starting and finishing, allocating responsibilities and the assembling of a group record in the form of a story book about the experience of the group. There are several examples of the development of our story company on the DVD. **(See extracts 23–37 on the accompanying DVD.)** As students progress through the inclusive storytelling programme, they will take on increasing responsibility for running the group. Roles will be shared out with different people taking them on for a designated period of time.

The eight Rs for group roles

1. **Registration** – one person checks the register and collects in the money for teas and coffees.

2. **Refreshments** – two people make tea and coffee each week and do washing up.

3. **Room management** – helping to set out chairs and tables, clearing away.

4. **Running activities** – as people become more familiar with the games we play, they can start to choose a game, explain the rules and run it.

5. **Reporting** – each person needs to have the opportunity to report back from the small group to the large group.

6. **Review** – regular discussion of how the group is going, once or twice a term, with students taking the lead.

7. **Representation** – every time we do a presentation or a talk with the press or radio, there should be someone from the group there, or their words represented.

8. **Rules** – everyone is responsible for checking that the rules set by the group have been followed.

Section 3:
Organising and delivering an inclusive storytelling programme

3.1 Before you start: planning

When you are planning your inclusive storytelling work, you need to prepare by:

- talking to key people
- sorting out finance
- getting your resources together
- finding a venue
- recruiting staff
- timetabling
- organising transport
- preparing information

Talking to key people

It is advisable to discuss what you are doing face-to-face with providers, to get their support in principle, and ideas for prospective applicants. It is also worthwhile to explore local strategic priorities for providers of services – for example, storytelling has obvious benefits in supporting person-centred planning.

We found that the idea of storytelling was very strange to many people. However good your initial information, you will encounter prejudice and misunderstanding. The term 'storytelling' means different things to different people. Some thought of it as childish, essentially to do with nursery rhymes and fairy tales (a local Head of Service remarked: *'at first I thought it was a bit Jackanory: I've changed my mind now!'*); one parent and one service user interpreted it as 'telling stories', ie fabrication and lies; another parent consistently teased his adult offspring about doing something 'babyish'.

We did think about renaming the inclusive storytelling programme as something like 'narrative skills' – but decided to stick to our guns, because what we are doing is definitely storytelling. Once our students had been coming for a few weeks, the people they lived with started to notice the benefits of increased confidence, and ability to talk about what had happened. Keep regular lines of communication, if possible having the home phone numbers. This is particularly important if you want to organise trips out to story circles or festivals.

The people we needed to consult before setting-up were:

- service managers and staff in centres and work preparation teams

- carers in residential homes

- social workers, psychologists and speech therapists – make sure that you know about arrangements for annual reviews so that you can contribute a report or attend if appropriate, and to make sure you are in the information loop so that no-one suddenly organises an important event for a student on a storytelling day

- administrative staff – if you can get agreement and support for an administrator to co-ordinate all the arrangements, this will ease things considerably

- relevant voluntary organisations

- further education college (who may well put the inclusive storytelling programme on with you)

- schools (if you are wanting to involve students as volunteers, or students with special needs themselves in the inclusive storytelling programme)

- partnership board

- advocacy groups

- your nearest storytelling group or circle

We communicated with families of the people we recruited after we had offered them a place, so that we did not raise expectations (or anxieties!). Preparing a leaflet about your plans, which sets out what the benefits will be for participants, is really helpful. It is also sensible to draw up a contract with service providers so that you have commitments from both sides in writing. Completed risk assessments may also prove useful.

Finance

You need to consider:

- remuneration for staff who are delivering the inclusive storytelling programme
- rent for the premises
- administration costs
- funds to enable people to attend at least one or two storytelling circles or events
- resources
- refreshments (we asked people to contribute a small amount each week which covered the costs, and allowed us to plan end of term parties)

Resources

A variety of different media are essential to support learning and develop communication. Resources for this inclusive storytelling programme should be supplied by the inclusive storytelling programme providers, and comprise:

- video camera
- monitor or data projector
- digital camera

The following resources are needed for immediate playback of activities to promote self-reflection and group feedback, and for recording purposes:

- flip chart
- drawing and writing materials
- portfolios – ring binder files in which people will record and keep their work
- sets of materials to support storytelling:
  - collections of magazine pictures
  - sets of play figures – knights and ladies, pirates, animals. Useful because many people will not actually know what a knight or a pirate looks like. Can be used for inventing stories, acting out and games.
  - simple costumes – hats are useful
  - musical instruments
  - coloured material – gauze or cotton
- CD player
- beautiful object to pass round in the closing circle
- talking stick

Venue

You may be lucky enough to find a home within a college or organisation. If you have to find your own accommodation, we found we needed the following amount of space:

- a large meeting room, big enough to allow all your students, trainers and volunteers to move around freely and work quietly in small groups. You may also want to invite an audience in at certain points during the year

- a kitchen area

- accessible toilets, reasonably near to your meeting room

- a small room for tutorials or for people to chill out

Try to find a space in the community if possible, but beware of draughty church halls or places that are so remote that you can't rush out and buy Blu Tack® or milk when you find you have run out! You are looking for somewhere that feels both prestigious and comfortable.

Staffing

Staffing levels are calculated with reference to the strengths and needs of learners in cognition, communication and social awareness, taking account of the need for intensive work in small groups to build up confidence and skill. We have found the minimum ratio to be one staff member for a group of four learners who have special educational needs or learning disabilities.

If you are planning to deliver an accredited course, you need to ensure your staff have the appropriate experience. The following recommendations are drawn from the course materials.

The ideas in this book are designed to be taught by people with essential skills and experience in:

- telling stories in a public forum

- teaching or running workshops for children or adults who have special educational needs

They need to demonstrate knowledge of the following:

- a range of traditional stories

- the culture of inclusion and participation

- disability awareness

It is useful if at least one trainer can offer skills in a complementary art form such as graphic art or music.

The trainers may be backed up by support staff (eg volunteers, carers) who will operate as part of the team. We were lucky enough to have a member of social service staff seconded to us, who took responsibility for managing health needs, knew many of the group and so could help them remember experiences. Students who have successfully completed an accredited course in storytelling might take on training or support roles as appropriate.

There should always be someone on the premises who is qualified in first aid, and who is fully aware of the relevant health and safety guidelines and procedures which operate locally. For example, you should have readily available an incident record form, and if people take medication you should have a form for each day to record that this has been taken.

All staff who are involved in delivering inclusive storytelling should attend a training day prior to the commencement of your planned activities. Planning is needed throughout – we built in a half-term break where staff met without students, and we also met for one day before the activities and sessions began, and one day after each term finished to review and plan the next term's work (six days in total).

Timetabling

Deciding on which day to run your inclusive storytelling sessions is critical. Many prospective students will have extremely full lives and commitments, so that negotiation with them and their key workers and families at the recruitment stage is very important. Bear in mind that storytelling days are full and tiring, so as well as checking their daytime commitments, make sure you do not clash with other activities such as regular social clubs or sport. Holidays can be problematic – we had one student who went away regularly during the term without informing us. Unless absolutely unavoidable, you do not want people to either leave early or come late, as this is very disruptive. Keep to the same day for the full year, and timetable half terms. If you have volunteers or seconded staff, make sure that they can attend team meetings on the half terms. You will probably need to meet with the core team members also at the end of the term and before the beginning of the next term in order to keep on top of the paperwork.

Arranging transport

Transport is probably the single most difficult problem you will encounter if, like us, you are drawing people from a wide catchment area. You should negotiate for the provider organization (social services, voluntary body or education authority) to arrange it, but try to get the mobile numbers of the regular drivers, so that should someone fail to arrive, you can get onto them straightaway. Make sure all drivers have your timetable for the year with start and pick-up times clearly marked, that you remind them of half term breaks and the dates the inclusive storytelling programme starts again. Have backup plans for when transport fails to pick someone up at the end of the day.

Information

Prepare a brochure, with the following information:

- names and photos of trainers, with a bit about your background

- names of participants

- address and photo of venue

- timetable of the inclusive storytelling sessions, with all the relevant dates, including outings if you know them in advance, party dates

- outline of a typical day, including start, finish and break times

- contact numbers, particularly for administration; your mobile number for emergencies on the day

- your procedures for health and safety

- aims and outcomes of the inclusive storytelling sessions

- what you expect from participants (eg punctuality, confidentiality, commitment, willingness to try new things) (the contract)

- what you undertake to provide for them (listen to them, act on their concerns, support, teaching) (the contract)

- transport arrangements

- what to do if they do not want to continue with the inclusive storytelling programme

During the inclusive storytelling sessions, if you have to send letters home, send duplicates to key workers or centre/home staff; often people will not realise or will forget what to do with a letter.

3.2 **Recruiting students**

The inclusive storytelling activities and ideas in this book are designed particularly with the needs of young people and adults who have learning disabilities or special educational needs. In principle it is open to anyone who feels it would be appropriate to their own stage of learning and interest.

Age-range

At one point the ages of the people in the group ranged from 18 to 80. In practice we found this was a bit too demanding for the youngsters who had only just left school – they really wanted to be with other young people. However, our 28-year-old was perfectly at home with the older folk in the group. We therefore suggest that you need to consider experience as well as age when planning for the group – people who have been out and about will perhaps have more tolerance.

Advertising the inclusive storytelling sessions

You will need to advertise the inclusive storytelling sessions well in advance. You can write and circulate leaflets in accessible and easy to read formats, but we found the best approach was to run a series of short taster workshops where we told a traditional story, played a couple of interactive games and then asked if anyone would be interested in the inclusive storytelling programme, or (so as not to raise expectations too much) a half-day workshop. This was easy to arrange within day centres, but more difficult at work preparation centres where people often went out to a work placement or were committed during the day. We negotiated times before the day began, at the end of the day, or during lunchtimes. Try to find a time when everyone is getting together for a meeting, and where they can spare you half an hour to run the session. When you talk to service providers you can also give them referral forms. See Appendix 2.

Preliminary workshop

Once you have a list of people who in principle would like to attend your inclusive storytelling sessions, you may want to run a preliminary workshop. You will find information for running a preliminary workshop and assessment in Appendix 3. We had about 35 people interested in storytelling, and two trainers ran a series of half-day workshops to make sure we had people who could really cope with the demands of the inclusive storytelling sessions.

The workshop consisted of:

- an introductory game
- a story told by the trainers, with opportunities for joining in
- a follow-up activity from the story, in small groups
- a pair activity where people told each other something about themselves
- a closing activity

Ideally, criteria for attending the inclusive storytelling programme are as follows:

- enjoyment of stories, evidenced through engagement, laughter, positive feedback
- ability to listen to and understand a short story: comprehension level equivalent to at least three information carrying words
- awareness of the needs of others, and the ability to adapt behaviour to meet those needs
- expressive language in speech or sign or augmentative communication at least equivalent to two information carrying words. (Speech and language therapists assess how many key words in an instruction or piece of information can be decoded and expressed by the student. For example 'Give me the purse and the key' involves three information carrying words. (See: www.derbyshire-language-scheme.co.uk)

After the workshop, trainers record comments on the presence or absence of each skill, and the amount of support required to enable the person to engage with the range of activities. A preliminary record form to record your observations can be found in Appendix 4.

Those who fulfil the basic requirements are sent a letter of acceptance and an invitation to interview (see Appendix 5) designed to make the information accessible with large print, plain and simple language and graphic support. Individuals who cannot read the form are invited to go through it with a relevant facilitator (key worker or family). Staff can follow up an application with each participant by phone, usually with the key worker, advocate or family member. This contact is used to:

- check if the individual would like to attend the inclusive storytelling programme and arrange a preliminary interview

- determine outcomes for people who would like to come, but have not met minimum requirements

For prospective students, a preliminary interview is held with the student, trainer and key worker/advocate or family member. See Appendix 6. This interview is used to:

- ascertain the commitment of the student, by going through information about the planned inclusive storytelling programme and what the student can expect, providing contracts (see Appendix 7) and going through them together

- ascertain any needs (eg communication, literacy, diet, health, hearing, medical – (see Appendix 8), which you can make accessible with graphics if necessary, or use existing profiles which provide similar information. The forms should be kept on file during the programme.)

- discuss necessary arrangements (eg transport; holiday dates)

- obtain consent for video recording (use forms available in your districts)

- answer any queries

Before the inclusive storytelling sessions begin, the student is sent a welcome letter and brochure.

Students who do not fulfil the criteria

Of course it is difficult to turn people down – however, it is really important to make sure that people do not undertake something that is inappropriate, and fail later down the line. Following the preliminary workshop, or other referral, trainers can discuss with key workers what alternative activities are available, and courses which students might attend in order to develop relevant skills which might enable them to apply in a subsequent year (for example, a social skills or communication course). Trainers then write a letter to the individual to inform them of these options and to suggest that they should discuss them with the key worker. They can also be told that their contact details will be added to a database for invitations to any workshops or public performances that they might like to attend.

Exit strategy

Despite these efforts, it may be the case that people find the inclusive storytelling sessions do not suit them after a few weeks. Make sure that you have planned for exit interviews in which, for example, you will identify with the student what they liked, what they did not like, and what they will be doing instead. Provide this information in an accessible form for them, and make sure that all relevant people are informed. It is useful to have a key worker or staff member present at this interview.

3.3 Running the sessions

Make sure you plan the day so that you always follow a similar structure. Try to involve your students as quickly as possible in helping with the organisation. We operated a rota to make sure that people took turns at ticking the register, putting up the order of activities for the day, making tea and coffee and leading the feedback. As they become more confident and familiar with the activities, they can begin to lead warm up games and discussion. Figure 2 provides an example of a structure for the day.

Figure 2 **Structure of the day**

Timings	Activities	Strand
9.00–9.45	Planning and set up	
9.45–10.15	Registration Tea and coffee Chat	Story company
10.15–10.30	Check in Register News (**See extracts 28–30 on the accompanying DVD**) Announcements Order for day	Story company
10.30–10.45	Warm-up game	Story company (**See extracts 23–25 on the accompanying DVD.**)
10.45–11.00	Story giving major theme for the day	Story theme (**See extracts 3 and 12 on the accompanying DVD.**)
11.00–12.00	Group work	Story skills (**See extracts 3 and 15–17 on the accompanying DVD.**)
12.00–12.30	Large group – report back, games, performance, sharing, songs	Story skills
12.30–1.30	Medication Lunch break (**See extract 34 on the accompanying DVD.**) Tutorial time, art work Portfolio work	
1.30–1.45	Large group game, activity, story, or song	Story company
1.45–2.45	Small group work and storytelling by students	Story lines Story skills (**See extracts 4, 10 and 18 on the accompanying DVD.**)
2.45–3.00	Tea break	Story company
3.00–3.20	Feedback and announcements	Story company (**See extract 36 on the accompanying DVD.**) Feedback circle
3.20–3.30	Closing activity	Story company
3.30	End (**See extract 37 on the accompanying DVD.**)	
3.30–5.00	Review, qualitative assessments and future planning	

When you plan work for a term, try to make sure that all the strands are covered through games and specific activities. Figure 3 provides detail on the skills that can be covered and Figure 4 provides an example of how to plan the skills into a period of work.

Figure 3 **Story skills**

Structural	Feelings	Social	Language
Memory and sequencing Who, what, where, why Setting information: where, when Building a climax to a story Conclusions and resolutions	Using facial expression Intonation Gesture Pausing, rhythm and stress In the manner of the word	Gaining attention Maintaining attention Eye contact Posture Control of story space Finishing and getting out of the space Listening and attention	Range of verbs, adjectives, nouns, Sentence structure – past tense, hypotheticals Conventions of stories – metaphors, similes etc

Figure 4 **Cycle for story skills: term 1**

Week	Skills			
	Structural	**Feelings**	**Social**	**Language**
1	Introduction			
2				
3				
4				
5				
6				
7				
8				
9				
10	Performance			

Staff rota

We rotated tasks among trainers, with one person telling the key story, one person responsible for administration and time keeping, and one person keeping notes in a diary of particularly interesting comments, behaviours and issues (this is vital if you are doing the accredited course, since a lot of observation is called for). If you have enough staff, it is very useful to have one person on emergency duty to look after people who are taken ill, or become upset, or need time out. Make sure there is always a qualified first aider on site. Always take time at the end of the day to discuss what happened and make notes, if necessary readjust your plans for the following week.

Organising news sessions

We found that people were really keen to share their experiences of the week, but that there were a few problems associated with this activity. One was that they really wanted (like all students!) the attention of trainers, rather than fellow students; another was that once given the floor, people tended to start at the beginning of the week and go right through, rather than selecting information. This meant that the news session started to take up half the morning. So once people knew each other a little better, we ran it in a different way, by splitting people into carefully structured groups of three or four, and asking them to tell each other their news in ten minutes. The group then appointed a spokesperson to share the main events with the whole group, in a five minute report session. The spokesperson had to start with the news of others, and end with his or her own news. We withdrew during the group discussions and only returned for the report session. This was extremely successful in promoting relationships and chat. Volunteers and other staff members could be on hand, but were trained not to take over the group, to defer to the group members, and support others where needed to tell their own news (they of course shared their own main events within the group as well). **(See extracts 28–30 on the accompanying DVD for examples.)**

Group cohesion

In the first weeks, we had a lot of discussion about:

- aims and hopes for the group

- group rules, which everyone signed up to.

See extract 33 on the accompanying DVD.

We did this in small groups, then wrote the rules out with accompanying symbols, and in the first term we had these pinned up and went through them quickly at the beginning of the day. The ideas we came up with are listed in Figure 5.

Figure 5 **Hopes, fears and group rules**

Fears and how to cope with them

Ghosts and scarey stories talk about facing fears;
going away with something that makes you feel strong;
say if you want a story to stop

Communication understanding each other
(use gesture and sign, say if you don't understand)

Being ill and missing ring up and tell the person what happened
(share phone numbers)

Getting tired say you need a break

Feeling shy 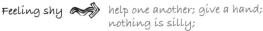 help one another; give a hand;
nothing is silly;
if you feel you want to say something, you will be listened to

Remembering new things don't worry, ask to have it again,
make a note

Talking in front of other big groups we will do things together,
you can always 'pass'

New different things 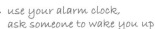 be brave

Forgetting things have a diary

Waking up on time use your alarm clock,
ask someone to wake you up

See extract 31 on the accompanying DVD.

Group rules

Not going out of building without telling someone

Not talking too long – we will use a wind-up gesture to let you know if you need to finish!

Fire – have a fire drill, make someone responsible for this

Don't run

Passing activities that you are not comfortable about

Careful with hot drinks

ONLY TWO PEOPLE IN THE KITCHEN AT ONE TIME

Confidentiality – what is said in the group stays in the group, ask if you want to tell someone's personal story

Protocol for talking – use a 'talking stick'

Respect through listening – don't interrupt

Using cards – I can't understand, can't hear

TELLING PEOPLE, IF YOU CAN'T HEAR, DON'T UNDERSTAND

Going to loo, or sitting down – do this when you need to

One person talks at a time

Don't say unkind things – be supportive

See extracts 32 and 33 on the accompanying DVD.

Rituals

Each group develops their own symbolic rituals, perhaps with special objects, songs, activities that are repeated each week and come to stand for something that is shared and particular. In our case we developed the idea of the Siege Perilous – a special seat kept at Arthur's court for the Knight who was to come, the perfect knight. In the legend, if the wrong person sits in the seat they go up in flames. We had a lot of jokes about the Siege Perilous, but it also stood for something important – the place we keep in the Company for those who have left us and those who are to come. **(See extract 35 on the accompanying DVD.)**

Team games

Some people find team games stressful, particularly if winning and losing are involved. I learned a more robust attitude from a 'Wolf and Water' week-long course where the competition was incessant and fierce and a lot of fun (see: www.wolfandwater.org). With the Unlimited Company of Storytellers we developed a fun approach which involved pitting teams (usually identified by colour) against each other, but ending up giving everyone points. No-one cared! It is also useful because if people are finding aspects of a game difficult they can score or be a judge. **(See extract 15 on the accompanying DVD.)**

Portfolios

Each person on the inclusive storytelling programme should have their own ring binder in which to collect: the story of the day (written up simply, with symbols if you can manage it and these are needed); their own illustrations; their own personal stories; photographs, postcards and artifacts gathered on holiday or visits. **(See extract 7 on the accompanying DVD.)** We worked on these during the time after lunch, when people could sit and draw or dictate to someone, and during targeted sessions in the day as appropriate. Our group were very proud of their portfolios, and often worked on them at home.

If you are doing the accredited course, it is better to keep all the forms you need for evidence separately – some people may not be very good at remembering their portfolios, and there is nothing worse when you come to collate the evidence than finding you are one form missing and the person concerned is on holiday!

Storytelling by students

Right from the start, plan a short session (15 minutes maximum) where the students themselves will tell stories. It is a good idea to do this in pairs, initially with staff support. Use the collaborative storytelling approach that you will find described in Section 5. Make sure everyone has a turn. You can practise with the students during tutorial time, or at another point in the day. Students can start by telling any story they like – traditional, film or TV, book. By the end of the inclusive storytelling programme, they should be researching and telling traditional stories from different cultures, to expand their own story knowledge. During the final term, they should be spending part of the time working on their own story to tell at a performance. You may want to suggest these stories. Help them to make links between the story and their own experience – possibly even to tell a personal narrative that the story makes them remember. **(See extract 4 on the accompanying DVD for a personal story linked to Ceridwen's Cauldron.)** Record onto separate tapes for each student – that way all the evidence will be kept together. Students may need quite a lot of help to move from basic memories, perhaps generated by photographs, into real narration. **(See extracts 5–6 and 12 on the accompanying DVD.)**

Discussion and feedback sessions

We found the group were very supportive at giving feedback to people who had told stories. We used the well-tried formula – something good, something you might change, what we all enjoyed about your telling. **(See extracts 19–22 on the accompanying DVD.)**

Lunchtimes

Informal chat was a very important development for our group. At first they would often sit and wait for trainers – but by the end of the year, they were chatting to each other. You can assist this by engaging in relaxed spontaneous chat in a collaborative way during breaks. **(See extracts 6 and 34 on the accompanying DVD.)**

Closing feedback

We used a lovely glowing ball to pass round at the end of the day and asked people for one or two comments about how the day had gone. If people went off track, we would gently remind them that we were just talking about today. We asked students to lead feedback sessions in turn. **(See extract 36 on the accompanying DVD.)**

Dealing with difficulties

Some of the problems our group encountered were: people who talk too much and don't listen; people who find it hard to sit still or who persistently fiddle; people who were very affected by a particular story; people feeling ill or upset; arriving late because of transport difficulties (by far and away the biggest problem). It is really important to tackle problems directly and quickly. When these were problems relating specifically to how people told stories or interacted, we tried first to work with them with the whole group. If you have worked together in depth on the group rules this will be easier. **(See extracts 31–32 on the accompanying DVD.)**

We dealt with personal problems by:

- having a small 'chill-out' space where people could relax, with a CD player, drawing materials, and sets of small play figures (these were particularly useful for one person in our group, who calmed down when she manipulated the figures and used them to act out a story)

- ensuring one trainer was available as a carer or supporter for people who needed it

- using tutorial time after lunch to talk over persistent problems with the people concerned – asking them what difficulties they were having, gently pointing out the problem if they were not aware of it, and getting their own ideas for a management plan; worst case you may have to discuss with them whether the inclusive storytelling programme is appropriate to their needs at the moment, and whether they should leave

- making sure you have contingency plans for referring people – take the name and number of key workers, write up incidents immediately and inform social services, write reports on persistent concerns and follow through

Reactions to stories

You simply do not know what buttons will be pressed by powerful stories, which deal inevitably with big emotions – love, grief, anger, jealousy, power. Always be aware of people's reactions to stories, and make sure you talk about how the story makes you feel. You may need to take time out to do more therapeutic work with the story – using music, art, and clay were media we found very useful. Some good books on therapeutic storytelling can be found in the resources list.

Visitors

Once the group feels cohesive and comfortable, do encourage visitors. They are great morale boosters and offer real opportunities for the group to show what they can do and practise their skills. Make sure people sign a visitors' book and write comments – these are very useful as evidence for progression, for the success of the group and for funders.

Refreshments, parties and celebrations

For coffee and tea breaks we asked for a small contribution per week, and used this for refreshments – making sure we had fruit as well as the ever-popular biscuits. We always had an end of term event to which friends, family, staff and visitors could be invited. Food is essential, but plan this – for our first Christmas party we just invited people to bring a contribution, and ended up with a waist high tower of packets of mince pies.

Visits out

It is really important to try and ensure that everyone gets to visit a local storytelling event. You can find out about local circles and festivals from the Society for Storytelling webpage (www.sfs.org.uk), and your local library and arts centre should also have information. Check out beforehand that the organisers are prepared to welcome people with disabilities and that the venue is accessible (most circles seem to be up steep flights of stairs in pubs, and involve sitting on tiny stools). Consider funding for this before the inclusive storytelling programme starts – for everyone to go to two events you may need up to 10 or 12 trips (don't try and take everyone to your local circle, just two or three at a time), and you may need to think about costing in your time as well as the cost of tickets, refreshments and transport. Visits are a great morale booster and a way of getting people known in the local community, and they provide a natural way for people to hear and learn more stories. We always told in the group one or two of the stories we had heard.

Finding stories

The Internet is your best source of stories. Section 8 provides some good websites. Also look at the Andrew Lang series of fairy tales, which come from all over the world, and use your local library.

It is etiquette among storytellers to credit the person who has told you the story or where you found it, if it is not published, or taken from a personal website.

Section 4:
Games

We include warming up, opening and closing games within the strand of story company – although they also have an obvious relevance to story skills. This is because we have found their main function is to set expectations and act as familiar rituals to start and end the day.

4.1 Warming up

Physical and vocal warm-ups are very important for getting the body moving, and the voice warmed up (See extracts 23–24 on the accompanying DVD.)

Get your stance right – Nick Hennessy, a well-known storyteller who has helped us, suggests standing with feet parallel, knees slightly bent, and arms loose. This is the neutral position for telling, from which you can move easily. Do simple bending, stretching, arm swinging, reaching forwards, backwards and sideways. Use music to help you. There are many ideas for warm-ups on the Internet, or in yoga, martial arts and dance manuals. See for example: www.renfaire.com/Acting/physical.html

4.2 Voice work

Storytellers need to learn to breathe and speak using the diaphragm, and to project their voices using the appropriate pitch, rhythm and volume.

- Breathe out as far as you can. Then take a breath and make a sound – 'ah', 'mm'. Keep it going as long as you can. Make short sounds then long sounds.

- Experiment with different sounds. Create a sound pool – everyone drops a sound into the pool.

- Use gesture to show the difference between loud sounds (hands move apart) and quiet sounds (hands move together), high sounds (hands move up) and low sounds (hands move down).

- Make quiet sounds, then loud sounds. Conduct an orchestra to show the sound getting louder then softer again. Take it in turns to do this. Now use single words. Discuss the difference between speaking loudly and clearly and shouting (which is not a good idea).

- Project your voice to the opposite end of the room, looking ahead and sending your voice on a journey. Then play a name game and put this into the context of a story – we are on a voyage when the ship begins to sink. We leap into the sea, and one by one are rescued into two different lifeboats far from each other. Call names: split into two lines, one with its back to the other at opposite ends of the room. Each person calls the name of someone in the opposite line, taking it in turns. When a person hears their name, they turn round. When the whole line has turned round the first line turns its back and the exercise is repeated.

See extract 24 on the accompanying DVD.

4.3 **Opening games**

Opening games function as social warm-ups: to get energy moving in the group, to help people to get to know each other, to reduce anxiety and to break up habitual seating patterns. (**See extracts 25–27 on the accompanying DVD** which illustrate three opening games popular with our group.) They should last about 10–15 minutes only; some can be expanded to cover some of the story aspects. Health and safety is paramount here. It is really important to organise and agree group rules for games (rules for running, care to provide space) and for physical contact – agree between yourselves where people will touch each other (shoulder, arm, thigh).

Debrief

After each game, have a brief discussion to identify why we are playing the game – what does it do for the group, how does it help us tell stories? Some of our recurrent suggestions are: teamwork, energy, turn-taking, and communication. Some of these games will also be useful when working on story skills – the difference is that rather than just a focus on warming up, you are specifically setting out to develop a particular area.

4.4 **Name games**

These are designed as very quick icebreakers.

- **Name intro** – Everyone says their name accompanied by a gesture, which is copied by the whole group, OR 'and I like (category example: TV, food, pet, sport)' OR 'and I'm a (story character: princess, witch, knight, king, beggar, soldier).' Everyone reacts accordingly.

- **Ball park** – Say the name of a person in the group and throw them the ball. A variation is to say the name and then throw to someone else; have two balls on the go at once.

- **Get that name** – One person stands in the middle, and says the name of someone else, who swaps with them. A variation is Plum Plum Plum on page 60.

- **Name swap** – One person stands in the middle and says two names. Those people have to swap places, with the middle person trying to get into a space before they do.

- **Name clap** – The leader claps three times and then says a name (clap, clap, clap, John). That person takes up the rhythm and continues. The rhythm must not be broken.

- **Name dice** – One person throws a large dice, counts round the group the number that is on the face and says the name of that person, who then throws.

- **Greeting** – Everyone walks briskly round the room, greeting each person that they meet by name. Make this more elaborate by trying out some different ways of greeting: bow and curtsey, high fives, Masonic handshakes or salutes.

- **Who stood where?** – If the group is very large, do this in teams. One person stands in the middle and looks round. They then shut their eyes and try to remember by pointing who was where. People who are named correctly stay in, people who are misnamed sit out. At the end, see who is left. You can start with small groups of four and then build up.

- **Who's talking?** – One person is blindfolded and sits in the centre. Others approach in turn and say 'Hello' or a longer sentence. The blindfolded person guesses who it is – if they are right, they swap places. Move on to 'squeak piggy squeak' where the person just makes a noise.

- **Whose shoes?** – Half the group line up behind a sheet, so that only their feet are visible. The other half stand in front of a person behind the sheet and have to guess who it is.

4.5 Non-verbal games

These games are not only good for people who have difficulty talking, but also for developing timing, co-ordination and non-verbal expression.

- **Pass the clap** – Stand in a circle. One person starts by turning to the person next to them and clapping once in their direction, making eye contact as if passing the gesture on. That person takes it and gives it to the next person. This is actually more difficult than it looks if it is done properly. *Variant:* suddenly change direction, or start sending it across the circle; speed it up and slow it down. **(See extract 26 on the accompanying DVD.)**

- **Pass the touch** – Very good for people sitting down. Using one finger, move it around and touch the finger or hand of the person sitting next to you. Introduce variations by moving the finger up and down, behind you, throwing something up in the air or taking something off your shoe, etc. Always end by passing it on. **(See extract 27 on the accompanying DVD.)**

- **Pass the football** – Using your feet, pass a large soft ball from one to another.

- **Pass the face** – One person adopts an exaggerated facial expression, draws a hand over their face and 'throws' the expression to someone else across the circle. That person must copy it and throw it to someone else. *Variant:* when people can do this, change the expression as you catch it and throw the new one on – eg smile changes to frown, frown to surprise. **See extract 13 on the accompanying DVD,** which shows an example of this game within the specific context of working on feelings.

- **Thunderstorm** – One person starts the storm by rubbing their hands together (wind rustling), which everyone copies. The leader then changes to quiet clapping or tapping knees for soft rain, which gets louder and quicker, finally thigh slapping, then stamping feet for thunder. The actions are then reversed until there is silence.

- **Follow my leader** – March to music around the room, with everyone following a leader and copying their movements. At a signal, the line turns round and the person at the back becomes the leader.

- **Copycat** – One person stands in the middle or at the front of the group and performs an action or gesture that everyone else copies. The next person takes a turn. At the end, try and remember all the gestures that everyone did. A variation of this is to have the person performing doing all the gestures in order before adding his/her own.

- **Build a mime** – One person stands in the middle or at the front of the group and performs an action. Whoever guesses first what it is goes into the middle and joins in with a related action, eg one person brushes their teeth, another goes up and washes her face, the next person starts putting on clothes. The game finishes when everyone is occupied.

- **Pass the pebble** – Everyone puts their hands behind their backs, sitting close together. One person stands in the middle, eyes closed. The pebble is held by one person who has to pass it to the next, without the person in the middle seeing it when they look up. The person in the middle looks up and points to where he thinks the pebble is. If correct, the holder of the pebble goes in the middle. A variation of this is to use a ring, threaded on to a long string, which people hold in their two fists in front of each other.

- **Balloon volleyball** – Group into fours, each with a balloon. The task is to keep the balloons as long as possible in the air. Note: a person who prefers to remain seated could take the role of umpire, checking-off how many times the balloon falls to the ground for each group.

4.6 **Verbal games**

The verbal demands here are pretty minimal and can be adapted to be even easier by using pictures.

- **Fruit salad** – Go round the circle, allotting fruit names (or pictures) – apple, orange, banana, pear, etc. When a particular fruit is called, those people must swap places. On the command 'Fruit salad', everyone moves. *Variant:* Minestrone – or anything you like! **See extract 25 on the accompanying DVD** which shows this game played as Minestrone.

- **Simon says** – Stand in a circle, or a straight line. One person is Simon, and calls out, or acts out, an action, preceded by the words 'Simon says', eg Simon says jump up and down; Simon says, pat your head. Every so often, the 'Simon says' instruction is left out. Anyone who carries it out is out of the game (or becomes Simon). 'Simon says' can be programmed onto a communication aid for people who are non-verbal.

- **Plum, Plum, Plum** – One person stands in the middle. Everyone chooses a fruit name. When the central person goes up to them and starts saying 'plum plum plum', the person addressed must say their fruit name before 'plum plum plum' is finished. Sounds complicated, needs quick reactions, but is actually good fun. *Variant:* people just say their own names.

- **Farmyard** – Show the group pictures of animals and check that everyone knows what sound they make. Divide the group in half and give out pairs of animal pictures. The two groups then start to make their sounds as loudly as they can, and each person must try and find their partner. Works well as a way of getting people into pairs. *Variant:* zoo, jungle, aviary.

4.7 **Memory and attention games**

- **I went shopping and I bought** – One person starts the game by saying one thing, the next person must repeat what the others have said before adding a new element. You can use pictures to support this. Make sure people with very poor memory go first. *Variants:* I went on holiday and packed..., I went to the zoo/jungle/safari and saw..., I went on a walk and met.... A slightly more elaborate version is one we use as an example of story structure work – See extract 8 on the accompanying DVD.

- **Chinese whispers** – Could introduce with the idea of rumour and gossip as a goddess of wind who blows around the world. First choose a word and send it round the group (write it on the flip chart and cover it up). At the end, write up the final word, reveal the first one and see how it has changed. Once the group are familiar with passing words, try a short sentence. Note: With people who have hearing impairments or speech difficulties, sit them next to a trainer and make sure that they are the start and end points, so that there is no communication breakdown. They can covertly sign their message as well.

- **Kim's game** – This game involves memorising a group of objects which are then covered by a cloth. Play this in teams, seeing who can get most, or play it as one group against the clock, keeping a record of how long it takes the group to remember everything.

- **See also:** Who's talking? Whose shoes? Who stood where? from the name games on page 57.

4.8 **Large group active games**

Provided you do have enough space and people are disciplined, there is nothing like these games for generating fun and energy. These games take more time, and can be developed further into complete stories by finding endings or resolutions and acting them out.

Games with one leader

In many of these games, one person is isolated and the rest of the group act together. If this is difficult for some people, the lead roles can be taken by two people together.

Using teams

All our group love team games and they are a great way of getting people to collaborate. We usually have the 'red' and 'blue' teams (because we can never find any other coloured pens). The teams change every time, and the essence is that both teams can get points, either for guessing right, or for having performed so well that the other team could guess, and nobody cares who wins in the end. Appoint a referee (who could be one of the group) who tells people what to do, when to do it, and allocates the points.

- **Pig, wolf, farmer** – Divide into two groups, with one referee. This is a variant of the old game *scissors, paper, stone*. Pigs (show curly tails with crooked fingers) catch farmers (who hold rifles), wolves (whose snapping jaws are shown by hands opening and closing) catch pigs, and farmers catch wolves. Each group decides what they will be, and at a signal, they produce their gesture. Whoever has the winning gesture pursues the others and tries to capture one of them. Stalemate, everyone just starts again. Keep a tally of how many points are won. *Variants:* giants, dwarves and elves

- **Postman's knock** – Everyone sits in a circle, with one less chair than there are participants. One person is the postman, and walks round the circle, carrying a letter. They drop the letter behind someone, and then run round the circle until they reach an empty chair. The recipient of the letter has to get up and run (or walk if this is safer) in the opposite direction, and try and get back to the chair before the postman. Can also be done by stamping on the floor, or knocking on someone's shoulder. Can be done with two postmen, but watch out for accidents.

- **Giant killer** – One person is the giant, and sits on the floor (or on chair) with a set of keys to the dungeon where his human prisoners are being fattened for the table. When he goes to sleep (ie closes his eyes) participants try to creep up without being heard and steal the keys. The giant is not allowed to open his eyes, but can point to whatever direction he thinks the thief is coming from. If correct, the thief must go back to his seat – unless he has already got the keys, in which case he goes to the dungeon! Can also be played by people disguising their voices to say a magic password to get past the giant. If the giant guesses who has spoken, swap places. For people with hearing problems, spread crackly paper on the floor.

- **What's the time, Mr Wolf** – One person is the wolf, and walks around the room. The rest walk behind him chanting, 'What's the time Mr Wolf?' The wolf pauses, turns round and says a time of day. When he says 'dinnertime', everyone runs for the farmyard (safe place). Non-verbally, can be shown with a cardboard clock face with moveable hands – 12 o'clock is dinner time.

- **Crossing the Nile** – Use a strip of cloth, or two chairs with a line between them, to represent the river Nile. On one of the chairs (or two people one on each chair) sits the crocodile who guards the crossing. In turn, people ask permission to cross, saying, 'Please Mr Crocodile, may I cross the River Nile', to which the crocodile(s) respond 'Only if you step really *adverb* (eg *fast, slow, high, low, big, small*)' or 'Only if you *verb* really well (eg *dance, hop, jump, run*)'. Non-verbally, the crocodile can be given prompt cards to show if necessary. Those who do it right can wade across, being careful to avoid the snapping jaws and flailing tail (you can also make 'stepping stones' with sheets of newspaper). The crocodile can challenge by saying that the person has not done it well enough, and they must swap places. At some point, the crocodile shouts 'flood plain' and everyone has to run across – anyone captured takes the place of the crocodile. Alternatives are that the crocodile says, 'Only if you bring me something *adjective* (eg *round, heavy, blue, square*)', or 'Only if you're dressed in *colour name*'. People may trick the crocodile by showing, eg that they have a red T-shirt under their blue pullover, or grey socks. Anyone challenged who does not have the right colour takes the place of the crocodile. This game can be turned into a longer story, by remembering the forfeits paid by each person, and trying to think of a way to outwit the crocodile, eg luring it away, putting a stick between its jaws, building a bridge, taking a boat.

- **Shipwreck** – Put sheets of newspaper and chairs around the room. One person gives the commands (which can be written on pictures). *Port* (left) *starboard* (right) *land ahoy* (shade eyes with hand) *clean the deck* (everyone sweeps and scrubs) *salute the captain* (everyone salutes) *heave ho* (everyone gets in a line and pulls) *shipwreck* (everyone must rush for a safe island). People who do not make it swap with the captain. Again, can be turned into a story game by inventing the details of the shipwreck and how you will get home again.

- **Sandstorm** – Get into pairs. One person is the head of the camel and the other is the hump, holding onto the front person's waist. Move around the room. The commands are *North, South, East, West* (to either end of the room and left and right); *palm tree* (both stand upright, with arms in the air) *tent* (two people make an arch for another pair to go under) *swap round* (head becomes hump and vice versa), *all change* (swap partners) *two humps* (pairs must split up and become the hump behind another pair) *sandstorm* (everyone must come into a tight circle, facing inwards). Story game can be developed by thinking about why you are crossing the desert, what you have in your saddle bags, where you are going, and who is chasing you.

- **Spaghetti race** – We adore this game. Divide into teams, sitting on chairs in straight lines one behind the other, with two facing chairs, or a long table. The referee provides the front person with a stick of long (uncooked) spaghetti, which must be passed back down the line. The last person brings the spaghetti out and places it on the facing chair or table. As he does so, everyone moves back. The referee then gives this person the next piece of spaghetti, and he sits down at the front and passes it back again. At the end of a designated time, whichever team has the most spaghetti wins. *Variant*: stick the spaghetti strands into something pliable eg to create a monster (note, this idea is derived from 'Spaghetti Head' on www.funattic.com).

4.9 **Games with objects and pictures**

- **Guess what's in the bag** – Unusual objects are placed in a bag, and people go round feeling and guessing what they are.

- **What's this?** – Divide into two groups, or pairs. Each group is given a few objects, and must think of gestures that represent how to use them. The other group has to guess what they are. Can lead into story activity (see display cabinet).

- **Touch blue** – Around the room, place objects of different colours. Show participants colour cards and make sure everyone knows what the colours are. When a colour card is shown, with the command 'Touch *colour name*' people must touch that colour wherever they can find it – on another person, or in the room.

- **Ice cream cone** – Put an ice cream cone (folded paper) in the middle of the circle. Each person in turn says something to go on the top and mimes putting it there (vanilla, chocolate, strawberry ice cream; toffee, walnut, cherry, choc flake, banana, raisins etc – can be done with pictures drawn from hat or box). At the end, everyone together goes through the list shouting 'I've got a vanilla, chocolate fudge, jam, banana ICE CREAM!' Everyone pretends to eat it and rubs their tums, saying 'yum yum'. Prepare for this if necessary by brainstorming suggestions first.

4.10 **Eye contact games**

These are good for encouraging people to look at each other and monitor eye gaze.

- **Wink/point murder** – Everyone draws a piece of paper from a hat, without showing what they have. One person is the murderer, and must catch the eye of someone else, and wink (or blink, or point) as covertly as possible. The victim must die as extravagantly as possible. The rest of the group try to work out who did it. If they don't know, the game is repeated.

- **Eyeball** – A ball is thrown between people just by making eye contact (silently).

- **Eye swap** – Swap places by making eye contact.

- **Guess what I'm looking at** – One person starts and looks at something in the room. The others have to guess what they are looking at by following the line of gaze. Whoever guesses right takes a turn. Non-verbal responses can be made by pointing, or going and touching the location.

- **Apple for the teacher** – One person is in the middle, with a group of objects or pictures. The others take it in turns to point their eyes to an object and then to a person, to indicate what must be given to whom. The recipient then goes in the middle. This game can also be played by gesturing or signing the function of the object.

- **Rabbits and foxes** – One person is the fox, in the middle of the circle, turning round slowly. One rabbit starts by making eye contact with another. This person must wrinkle their nose, show front teeth, scrabble with their paws or put hands above their heads as ears. If the fox sees it, he swaps with the unfortunate rabbit. Make it more difficult by outlawing repeat actions (ie each turn must be a different action).

4.11 Active games

- **Back-to-back race** – Get into pairs, standing back to back. Pairs walk quickly from one end of the room to the other. See who gets there first. (Can be paired with Plato's story of the origin of people, who were once circular and both male and female. Because of their arrogance, the gods split them in half, and now humans wander the world looking for their other half to complete themselves).

- **Knots** – Either in teams, or whole group with one person as the solver. The group get themselves into a tangle, linking arms and legs, lying on the floor or on chairs. The solver must gently untangle everyone.

- **Trust obstacle course** – In pairs or threes, one person is blindfolded and the other(s) lead them gently through an obstacle course. Do this non-verbally, just through touch, though it can be done by talking the person through it as well. At the end, talk about how it felt, and what worked best.

- **Tug of war** – Use a large rope or length of elastic material. Get into teams and see which team can pull the other across the room. Keep a score.

- **Rescue** – Get into pairs. One of the pair goes into the middle of the room – the sea – and at a signal, starts to 'drown'. Other partners must find ways of rescuing them within a given period of time (use egg-timer). They are not allowed to touch the other person, or make a sound, though the drowning people can be as dramatic as they like. Ways include – throwing a line, providing chair bridge, creating an island with newspaper, sending a boat (with a box). Make into a story by describing or showing the rescue.

- **Grandmother's footsteps** – One person is grandmother and stands at the end of the room with her back turned. The group has to move silently towards her. When she turns round, they freeze; if she sees someone moving, they are sent back to the beginning. The person who touches her without being seen becomes grandmother. Can be turned into a story game of get into the witch's or giant's castle.

- **Keys of the kingdom** – One person is the sleeping giant, with car keys on his/her lap. Others must creep up to take them. If the giant hears, he wakes up and the person is out. Successful thieves become the giant. Obvious story to embed this game into is *Jack and the Beanstalk*.

- **Frogs and lily-pads** – Played like musical chairs, only with sheets of newspaper. Instead of being out, everyone must come together on the last sheet, the task being to make the group as cohesive as possible (thanks to the Quaker *Alternatives to Violence Project* for this game).

- **Lay the table** – Groups of four. Each person draws (or is given) a plate, knife, spoon, fork (on separate pieces of paper). Task is to get into fours and lay the table correctly without talking (plate in the middle, knife on right, fork on left and spoon above or to the right of the knife). *Preparation* – show picture of place setting.

4.12 Identity games

These are games that take slightly longer than warm-ups, and help people to form relationships and get to know each other at a deeper level.

- **We're the same** – Draw two intersecting circles on the floor (or use hoops). Two people stand in the circles and the group tries to identify as many things as possible that they have in common. Can also be played with one person calling someone out to join them on the basis of a similarity, then that person chooses someone. Non-verbally, this can be done by pointing. Can be done as a way of pairing people off. *Preparation:* go round the group identifying some similarities.

- **I'm unique** – Everyone sits in a circle, with one chair in the middle. People take it in turns to sit in the chair, by identifying a characteristic or feature that is only true for them. Can be challenged by other group members, eg 'I go for a run at 7 every morning' – someone else may say 'So do I!'. The person in the chair then has to think of something else. You can keep a record of similarities and differences.

- **Identity collage** – Taking a pile of magazines, each person goes through them quite quickly and chooses five pictures that they find appealing to stick on a collage. We then look at the pictures and discuss why we chose them and what the images tell us about each other. Extension – next time you do it, make collage images for each other!

- **Name tag mania** – Participants are given a name tag and a magic marker. They are asked to print their name on the upper portion of the name tag and then to draw three objects that represent who they are on the bottom portion of the tag. After completing the activity, participants are then asked to share their names and what they drew on the tags (ie 'My name is Jess. I drew a sailboat, a dolphin, and a paint brush.') www.residentassistant.com/games/namegames

4.13 **Story games**

These are big games that take some time to play, but which have elements of warm-up, and are good for developing the idea of a story.

- **Come to see the king** – There is a king who is very, very, very evil. He is so bad that we have no option but to assassinate him (note, this game can be played more peacefully as a king who is remote from his people and guarded by unreasonable attendants). But he is totally paranoid and we have to provide a very convincing excuse as to why we should be allowed into his presence. Work in pairs or threes to create a back story for why you should pass. The guard needs to enter into some negotiation about this, not dismiss people out of hand, and should let in people whom he finds persuasive.

- **The sick princess** – The princess is lying sick in her bed, and we have to think of what will cure her. The princess may or may not wake up, depending on how well we describe or act the present we have brought.

- **The animals' problem** – A group of animals are faced with a problem – no food, a flood, hunters destroying their environment. They must work together to think of solutions.

You will find it easy to invent your own story games once you start – and there are more suggestions in the section on physical games.

4.14 **Closing games**

Closing activities function to complete the session, cement group dynamics and act as a bridge from the session to everyday life.

- **Takeaways** – Focus on gifts that can be taken from the session to support individuals in everyday life; they also affirm and support the development of group dynamics.

- **Angels** – Each person draws a small angel out of a bag, to represent a quality they might need or like to have – eg bravery, friendliness, hope. They present it to their neighbour.

- **Pretend presents** –The group leader takes suggestions of things that people would like as presents, and the group mime them. Each person then gives their neighbour a pretend present, gesturing and saying, 'Here is a lovely . . . for you'. The recipient responds with, 'Thank you for the lovely . . .'

- **Throw a smile** – Standing in a circle, each person smiles, takes the smile from their face and 'throws' it to someone across the circle, who catches it and puts it on.

- **Wish of the week** – Everyone in the circle identifies something they would like to happen this week. In response, the whole group cross their fingers, shut their eyes and say/shout, 'Good luck (name of person)'.

- **Sweet dreams** – Everyone thinks of a nice thing to dream about, draws it on a piece of paper and gives it to the person next to them/opposite. Alternatively, these can be mimed (like pretend presents) or can be pre-drawn pictures which are taken out of a hat (like angels)

- **Make a spell** – Pass a wand (real or imagined) round the group. Each person waves it and says a wish for someone else in the group.

- **Imaginary candle** – Pass around a pretend candle. The first person holds it and passes it to the next, who blows it out and lights a new one to pass on, or alternatively shields it carefully and passes it on.

4.15 **Affirmations**

Activities which reinforce a sense of individual identity/achievement, and make links with everyday life.

- **Say and do** – In turn each person goes into the middle of the circle and performs an action associated with something they do in the week (these can be identified beforehand). Everyone else copies the action, and guesses what it is.

- **'I liked it when you...'** – Each person in turn is the focus, and the group leader asks for suggestions of the best thing they have achieved in the group today. These can be written up on a flip chart.

- **The best bit** – Each person in turn says or mimes what the best bit of the day's activities has been for them.

- **Grow tall** – Each person in turn/or a pair goes into the middle of the group and crouches down/sits on a chair. The group together help the person to grow by blowing or lifting movements. This can be amplified by describing what is happening as the person gets taller – eg putting out shoots and leaves; stretching roots, unfurling petals, etc.

- **Happy feelings** – Going around the group, each person is told something really positive about themselves – eg I love your laugh; you draw well; you were really kind today. From a bag of confetti/rose petals/torn-up paper/bubbles, that person blows a little bit of themselves around the group.

4.16 **All together**

These activities reinforce a sense of the group as a whole, and the support it offers.

- **Group pat** – Everyone stands in a circle and gives a back rub or pat to the person in front; then turns round and does it the other side. **(See extract 37 on the accompanying DVD.)**

- **Dice hug** – Throw a large dice from one person to another. Take the same numbers of steps as are on the die face, first outward from the group (till half the group have thrown) and then back into the circle. End by holding hands or hugging each other.

- **Lift the sky** – Start crouching down, imagining grey clouds pressing down on the group. Everyone together puts their hands up at the same time, palms flat, 'One, two, three, lift' so that gradually the sky is raised. A bright yellow balloon can be floated and blown between people to end this game.

- **Energy fizz/firework** – Everyone crouches down, and one person starts a fizzing sound, which is taken up by each person in turn. At the end, everyone jumps up together, shouting 'lemonade' or 'rocket launch'.

- **Hot potato** – Everyone stands in a circle, facing each other's backs. At a signal, blow warm air between the shoulders of the person in front of you. *Variant:* Rub their back briskly.

- **Napoleon circle** – Everyone stands in a tight circle facing the back of the next person. At a given command, sit down on the knees of the person behind you. Should only be done with young fit people! (Note: this is supposed to have originated with Napoleon's Russian campaign in the dead of winter, to allow soldiers to rest without getting frost bitten bottoms.)

- **Musical instruments** – With a collection of instruments (can be odd objects) each person makes a sound, which is copied by the next person, who adds a new sound. At the end there should be a cacophony.

- **Spiders web** – A ball of wool is thrown around the group, with each person taking and holding a length of it, so that people are connected by a web pattern at the end. If there is time, this can be done by identifying connections between people – even as simple as who did you work with in the group today.

- **Group rounds** – Any round song can be used, or if not, catchphrases, eg a weather report. A third of the group start by saying, 'Wet and windy'. The next says, 'Freezing cold'. The next says, 'Warm and sunny'. Go round, getting louder, then fade out so that only one voice is heard. Can also be done with food – eg lollipops and ice cream/roast beef and Yorkshire pudding/spaghetti Bolognese, etc. The rhythms should be slightly different.

- **Conga** – The usual. Everyone forms up in a long line, and dances around the room. The group leader does an action which must be copied all the way down the line.

- **Indian ritual** – This is a traditional Native American dance which celebrates the Earth as mother. The leader has a tambourine, and sings the song *'Mother I feel you under my feet; mother I feel your heart beat. Hey ya hey ya hey ya; hey ya hey ya ho/hey ya hey ya hey ya, ho-oh-o'*. Everyone stamps in rhythm, going around in a circle. The pace of the song is quickened and gets louder ending with a triumphant cry. This is very good as a finale to the term.

- **Hail and farewell** – These are quick ways of saying goodbye and closing the session.

- **Hi fives Lo fives** – Go round the circle alternately giving a high five (hands slap at head level) and then a low five (hands at knee level). At the end, everyone slaps their hands together in the middle.

- **Hi and bye** – Form two circles, one facing inward, the other outward. The outer circle moves in one direction and the inner circle in the opposite direction. Shake hands and say, 'Hi and bye' to the person opposite you.

- **Syllabye** – Half the group whisper, 'Good' and the other half 'Bye'. Can be done first quietly then loudly/slowly then quickly/in different tones of voice.

- **Letterbye** – The letters that spell 'goodbye' (g-oo-d-b-y-e) are put on cards, enough for each person, and are drawn at random out of a bag. At a given signal, all the Gs go 'g', then the Os go 'oo', then the Ds go 'd', then the Bs go 'b', then the Ys go 'I' then the Es go 'er'. Do it really quickly and loudly.

- **Into the middle** – Everyone joins hands and runs to the middle shouting 'Goooood-bye!' **(See extract 37 on the accompanying DVD.)**

Learning to tell

Section 5:
Developing knowledge and skills

Knowledge of stories consists partly of how many different types of story you can tell, and the range of different types of stories you know. It may be helpful to introduce your inclusive storytelling programme by finding out what stories people already know, and developing their understanding of the range of stories that are told – story genre. Once a story genre has been explored you can progress to thinking about how stories are put together, work on how stories are told (emotional, social and language aspects), and use specific games to develop awareness of structural features. Figure 6 illustrates a systematic approach to work on storytelling skills and knowledge.

Figure 6 **Planning framework for storytelling skills and knowledge**

Introduction
Knowledge of stories
Story genres

How stories are put together
Story structure

How we tell stories
Games and activities to practise emotional, structural, social and language aspects

Review knowledge of stories
Being a storyteller

5.1 Story genre and knowledge of stories

The main types of genre we worked with were: ghost, love, fairy, detective, funny, adventure, legends, animal, historical, religious, news and personal. In the storytelling world it is very unfashionable to talk about fairy tales, the preferred term is wonder tales for any traditional stories involving magic and heroic characters. As our storytellers became more familiar with the culture, some of them began to use this term, but in a one-year inclusive storytelling programme you may find it easier to stick with what they know.

The following list covers most types of story. Some stories, of course, fall into more than one category. At the beginning of the course we did not rule out stories that were written rather than transmitted orally, since these are ones that people tend to be familiar with (eg *Peter Pan*, *Harry Potter*, *Titanic*, *Romeo and Juliet*).

One of the difficulties is understanding the difference between myths, legends, fables and wonder tales. In the storytelling world, absolute distinctions are made and are very important, since the whole point is to ensure that orally told stories are preserved. You will find that many story circles insist that only traditional tales are told, though some will allow personal-experience stories that could fall into one of the main genres. We found it better not to insist on this distinction and to let people tell stories they loved and were familiar with.

In broad terms the differences are:

- **Myths** – religious stories, concerned with the making of the world and the big questions of life and death, such as why we are here

- **Legends** – historical or semi-historical events or people, often located in particular places or countries; legends include hero tales, adventures, ghost stories

- **Wonder tales** – traditional fairy tales involving magic and transformation

- **Fables** – stories with a moral point or purpose, told to instruct and teach us how to behave; the characters are often animals with very human characteristics

The categories we used mix some of these up – for example, religious stories would include both classic myths (creation stories, the flood) and legends (Catholic saint stories, or tales of the Buddha). Our animal tale category covers fables. People found it fairly easy to understand legends (involving heroes like Robin Hood or Monkey). We also abandoned talking about fables in favour of 'animal stories'.

- Start by asking people in small groups or teams to think of all the stories they know. Write these down in a big list. Compare lists, count up how many – you will be amazed.

- Ask people to sort the stories into ones that go together – cut them up and put them on cards. Ask what are the differences between these types of story. Work up to the idea of categories. Now think of names for each type of story. This should lead you to the list of genres. Explain that not all stories can be easily categorised, but some stories have features which make them stand out as these types.

- Ask people in teams to draw pictures or find a gesture or noise to exemplify the type of story. For example, *ghost* – whooo! Waving hands; *love* – hands clasped above heart, flutter eyelids; *fairy* – wave magic wand. These will become your motifs to signal the type of story you are telling, so make sure you record them in some way. News stories we said were those about the real world that were broadcast on radio or TV. Personal stories were those we told about ourselves, friends and families.

- Now, in teams: brainstorm, write, draw or act as many features of key types as you can think of; *detectives* – crime, police, car chase, trial; *adventure* – hero(ine), far-flung location.

Once people are more familiar with the categories you can play some games, such as the following:

- **Guess the type** – Teams act out key features for others to guess the genre.

- **Story bingo** – Have bingo cards with the types drawn on them, using the motifs you designed yourselves. Have a list of cards with names of the different stories on them: *Sherlock Holmes, Titanic, Ghostbusters, Cinderella, Mahabaratha, Robin Hood, Monkey* (NB these must be the ones that people thought of themselves). The object of the game is to cover your bingo cards. People who are less aware of story genre can be the callers.

- **Links** – Lay out your story cards on the floor and have some coloured ribbon or string. Use this to make links between the stories, eg *Love stories and fairy stories* (hero and heroine fall in love, get married); *adventure and detective* (involve chase and villains); *animal and fairy* (animals appear in both, but only fairy tales have magic); *ghost and detective* (both are scarey).

- **That's wrong!** – Start to tell a story within one genre and introduce a feature that belongs to another story. Points to the teams who notice first. When people are familiar with this game, they can make up the challenges for the opposing team themselves.

If you want to work more specifically on knowledge of story, you can play similar games with the individual tales – eg changing the end of *Cinderella* to include *The Three Bears*, tell a story which brings in characters from as many different stories as possible, provide alternative endings to well known stories.

5.2 **Story skills**

We categorise skills into four aspects:

- **structural** (memory and organisation, genre)
- **feelings** (verbal and non-verbal expression of feelings and significance)
- **language** (or linguistic)
- **social** (or pragmatic)

Here are some ideas for working specifically on each of these aspects, which in turn are broken down into smaller components or behaviours. All are equally important.

Story structure

You have to develop a good memory to recall all the bits of a story, and you have to organise them in the right order. Stories begin with an attempt to get the listener's attention, and end with a phrase which hands over to the listener. We deal with these as social elements since they are to do with audience awareness. The basic elements of story structure are provided by 'wh-' questions. Story structure is often shown to be more complex than this, involving an introductory summary, resolution and coda, and in some models a central problem. For our purposes we worked with a much simpler format. (See extracts 8–12 on the accompanying DVD.)

- **Where and when did the story happen** – this is called setting. You don't always need both elements – when I was little; last Wednesday; a long time ago; in my village; at school

- **Who was in the story?** – the characters

- **What happened?** – the plot. The plot itself has its own structure – you need at least three events (beginning, middle and end) and the middle of the story needs to involve a climax or High Point, which the story builds up to. The ending involves some kind of resolution, which ties the story up, and 'hands it back' to the audience

- **Why?** Not only the motivation of characters, but what does it mean – the significance of the story to the teller and the audience. This is not always stated, but conveyed in the way the story is told. We usually dealt with this in discussion following a story, but it can be helpful if people state it at the end

By and large when **telling**, you start with *setting* elements, then *character*, then go on to *plot* (although an experienced storyteller can vary these). You also need some idea of *story genre*: that is the type of story that is told will set a framework for what you will find in the story. For example, ghost stories will usually involve a nighttime setting in a remote location, and involve characters from other worlds. In personal stories, genre is more to do with how it made you feel at the time of the experience – a story which is surprising, scarey, annoying, great, funny. The following activities start with the big picture, thinking of some different types of story, and then specific games for setting and character. Memory training is incorporated into the games, but for specific memory activities, consult opening games.

Start by discussing what goes into a story. A good way of doing this is to use a traditional rhyme that my grandmother used to say when I pestered her for a story.

> 'I'll tell you a story
> About Jackanory
> And now my story's begun.
> I'll tell you another
> Of Jack and his brother
> And now my story is done.'

This has some elements of a story – beginning, character, end, but is plainly unsatisfactory. Why? What's missing?

List what people suggest on the board. When you have a few, try telling a story that has ONLY these elements, and continue to ask what is missing until you have the full list.

Don't try to be too clever. We thought we were being very creative by suggesting the idea of a story cake, and the ingredients. The answers we got, though, were to do with sugar, flour, mixing bowls and spoons, and the image was just completely confusing. It took us about three weeks to unpick it.

We found that people readily identified the easy things – character and setting – they had more difficulty with plot, particularly the notion of the climax of the story, which is quite an abstract idea. Teachers/trainers did a LOT of short improvised stories, which just consisted of one routine event after another and asking if this was a good story, and if not, why not.

In the end, the term we came up with for what was needed in a good story was 'sparkle' – which bit of the story is the sparkly bit that is the most exciting and the reason why we tell it. You may find that the idea of building up to a climax can be illustrated in some other ways, eg pictorial visualisations of building up to climax.

On the whole, it is better to help people to think in terms of an interesting story with an exciting event in the middle, rather than getting too imaginative about how to represent the climax.

Once people have discussed the basic idea of how a story is put together, you can move on to some story games that exemplify the use of all of these features. You can use symbols that people are familiar with to help them recognise the features. Or the group can draw their own. Again, be careful with very pictorial illustrations: when we used a clock face for *when* people said 'clock'; if we used a castle to cue *where*, people said 'castle'.

- **Who, where, what, why...** – Set of cards with answers to these questions, plus set of question cards. One person turns up a question card, and asks the question – who was there? Where were you? What happened? Another has to pick an answer. You can also use a cube or dice with the questions on the faces. **(See extract 9 on the accompanying DVD.)**

- **Consequences** – Use the same cards to construct a story in two groups. Then one group tells their story to the other group.

- **Missing pieces** – All together, brainstorm key components of a story. Review story components. Each person hears a story with some key bits missing. They tick off on a chart what components are there and which are missing.

- **Play mat move** – Using a play mat or equivalent, the task is to move a figure round the mat, to directions given by other people. The group can then think together of things that happen to these people.

- **Display cabinet** – In two groups, with a set of objects for each group. The group has to think of how all the objects came to be together, making a story.

- **Detectives** – In one or two groups. The facilitator makes a tableau of a crime scene. The teams have to work out the clues to what has happened, and who did the crime. For example, picture of jewellery box open, nothing in it, large footprints leading to window, item of clothing dropped by window and blood on catch.

- **Object story** – A bag is passed round with a group of disparate objects. Everyone has to think about a way of bringing their object into the story. Advanced version: When a bell is rung, the person holding an object has to end the story appropriately - and the next person starts a new story.

- **What did I find?** – A bag with assorted objects is used, and each person takes something out to represent something found on a journey. Imagine how the object might help you on your journey.

- **I woke up one morning** – I went downstairs, I opened the door and saw a... lion, snow, flood, robber, film star, jungle, palace, garden. Act what happens next (can be done for one group by another, either as a task or to guess).

- **What happened?** – The group thinks of funny/dramatic/ scarey/happy events, and then of places or times where they might happen. Can be played in two teams – one group thinks of the event, the other of the location.

- **Tall tales** – Use the poem 'I saw a comet with a fiery tail...' or another fantastic tale. The task is to think of the most impossible event that you saw. After each one, the group responds with, 'Impossible. We don't believe you' and the teller replies 'It's perfectly true!' For people with limited verbal skills or who are non-verbal, they can pick a picture of an impossible event to go with a place – eg lion in a shop.

- **Props and pictures** – There are many traditions within storytelling which use pictures as an *aide memoire*: scrolls that unfold from India, screens like a portable cinema from Japan, and the Khavad, or storytelling cabinet which we built to use with our story. **(See extract 12 on the accompanying DVD.)** The main issue with using props and pictures is that these are aids to storytelling, not substitutes. They are not to be read like 'big books', but simply function in the background. The teller needs to look at the audience, not at the pictures.

Once people have got the basic idea that you have to include certain things in a story, you can play games to emphasise each of these.

Setting

- **Time and Place** – In teams, think of the most exciting way to start a story you can. One group takes time, the other, place. Toss a coin to see who starts. One person leads off with time and the other group contributes a place that goes well with it.

- **When I...** – The group complete sentences with this beginning (or have pictures that people choose in turn): *was little...was waiting for the bus...went on holiday...saw the doctor...was out shopping...went to hospital...went to the cinema...was having a bath....was looking out of the window... was in McDonalds...was talking to Paul..was going to bed...was watching TV.* This functions as a story starter – groups or pairs can develop the theme and find an ending.

- **When I was going to St Ives** – Using a bag with figures inside it, each person in turn takes something from the bag and says, 'When I was going to St Ives, I met a....' The figures can be retained to make up a story with, in pairs or small groups. (Linked story – Chicken Licken or other tales with serial meetings).

- **Story places** – Create a collage to show some different story locations – desert island, snowstorm, night time in the city. Think of appropriate stories that might happen there.

- **Weather words** – Show what the weather is like by acting it out – eg windy, rainy, cold, hot, muddy, snowing.

Characters

- **Puppets and pictures** – Puppets are an excellent way of working with characters – we made ours very simply from drawings on sticks. **(See extract 10 on the accompanying DVD.)**

- **Be a hero** – One group thinks of a set of characters which the other group must act – eg *dragon slayer, film star, judge, doctor, wise old woman, sick old man, jolly drunkard, miser, evil magician, giant, robber, good fairy, talking horse.* In its simplest form, the second group act them in turn for the first group to guess, with points being allocated.

- **Who am I?** – Development of the last game. The group think of a character and the second group mime something that they do in the story. Note: We played this towards the end of our inclusive storytelling programme, acting out members of the other team (in a kindly way! I was represented by someone rushing in the room panicking shouting where are my car keys?). *Advanced version:* Think of questions – or manner of the word activities – show us how you 'Clean your teeth?' or 'Are you very rich?'. Only 10 questions allowed. Can be narrowed down by choosing fairy tale characters who are discussed beforehand, with the whole group acting out how they would respond.

- **Hats and props** – Have a large sack of hats and simple props. People choose one and have to say or act the sort of person who would wear this – eg jester, king, ghost, farmer, businessman, starlet, milkmaid.

- **Characters in search of a story** – Each person gets a label pinned to their back: people treat them as the character – eg bowing to a princess, saluting a soldier. When they know what they are, they go to a particular location. *Variants:* Groups decide on the identity for the other group, and treat them in a particular way. OR Individuals pick identities and have to find someone from the same type of story and then go to a particular location: castle, battlefield, pub.

- **Why because...** – To explore character motivation. Buy this game, or make up reasons. Can be simple – eg why is the mother cross – because the son has not done the washing up, or complex, eg why does the snail have a shell for a house. Can be linked to 'Just so'– type stories.

Plot

- **What next?** – Start a story and ask teams to provide one or two events that happen next. Then experiment with working backwards, providing the ending for which they have to supply beginning and climax.

- **Puppets** – Using pictures and other devices is one way of supporting the correct sequence. Try to get the group themselves to decide how these will be used. (See extract 10 on the accompanying DVD.)

- **Wake me up** – Start a boring story, and everyone pretends to fall asleep. Someone must suggest an exciting event which will ensure that everyone pays attention.

- **Luckily, unluckily** – One person starts an event, eg a journey, and finishes with, 'Unluckily...' The next person invents an unfortunate incident, following it with, 'Luckily...' The next person invents a fortunate turn of event, but finishes with, 'Unluckily' and so on. If people do not understand these words, use *good day/bad day*.

- **The plot thickens** – Start a story and then invent multiple happenings and new characters. The person at the end has to tie everything together. (Note, this is really only suitable for people who really understand how to tell a story; many individuals are inclined to go off track anyway, and you don't want to encourage them).

5.3 Feelings

In the model of storytelling that we use, the ways in which feelings about the story are conveyed are absolutely central. This aspect of storytelling is the way in which the audience is cued as to the significance of the story. Without emotional engagement, the story will be lost. Both non-verbal and verbal ways of conveying feelings are included. Verbal features include direct reference to how people felt and judgements about events, people, places (eg *it was good, it was so hot, I was furious, well you can guess what I thought about that*); non-verbal include use of intonation, stress, repetition, showing engagement with the story, facial expression and gestures.

In discussion, tell a story with no animation and no non-verbal expression at all. Encourage people to consider what is missing and how the story could be improved. As storytellers, we use our voice, our faces, our hands and our bodies to help tell stories well.

Ask groups to think of all the different feelings they can, and the bodily, vocal and facial ways of expressing these. Then play some games to practise them. Several people in our group found this extremely hard – some folk may actually have neurological impairments affecting their ability to perceive and produce different facial expressions and intonation; others may have been so socially conditioned that their faces are permanently set in a smile; other folk who have autistic spectrum type problems may not perceive the significance of conveying feelings, or may find it difficult or threatening to do so.

Basic facial expressions

- **Picture this** – Using photos or pictures/symbols, first of all go round, getting everyone to imitate the expressions on the cards and talking about them. Then each person (or in pairs) picks a card and imitates the expression for others to guess.

- **Copycats** – Go round the group thinking of feelings. One person makes a face/body movement and takes it off themselves and throws it to someone else. They imitate it. Go all round the group and see if the expression you end up with is the same as the one you started with. *Advanced version* – They have to imitate the feeling and change it into a new one. **(See extract 13 on the accompanying DVD.)**

- **Opposites** – Same as above, but more demanding. The task is to produce an expression which is the opposite of the original.

Showing feelings with your voice

- **Feeling-word snap** – Put the feeling together with the word and say it in the appropriate voice, eg scared, angry. Can also be played by one person making the expression and another person supplying the word or vice versa. **(See extract 15 on the accompanying DVD.)**

- **How many ways can you say...** – Yes? No? Think of a set of questions – *would you like to...can you do...are you ...* Find how many different ways you can intonate yes or no, and discuss what meaning would be conveyed.

- **Voice the word** – The whole group together, then subsequently individually, say words in ways that convey their meaning, through the voice and adding gesture: *big, small, happy, sad, quick, slow, cold, hot, sleepy, strong, weak, bouncy, long, fat, thin, fierce, kind, sweet, bitter/ disgusting, beautiful, clean, dirty, wet, dry, prickly, smooth, rough, warm, funny, windy, tight, loose, scarey.* **(See extract 16 on the accompanying DVD.)**

Showing feelings with your body

- **Manner of the word** – Split into two groups. One group thinks of activities which must be done by the other group – eg *dig the garden, toss a pancake, clean your teeth, wash the window, lay the table, have a drink, run for a bus, do the ironing*. The second group thinks of some adverbs. They do the activity 'in the manner of the word' for the first group to guess (activities and adverbs can be supplied in picture or word form if necessary), eg *quickly, slowly, sadly, cheerfully, angrily, happily, loudly, quietly, calmly, frantically, frightened, bravely/heroically, tiredly, energetically, with a pain, clumsily, bored, excitedly*.

- **Animal magic** – First person chooses an animal to mime, then next person mimes this and changes it into something else. Whole group has to remember and copy the sequence.

- **Sound effects** – The use of voice and body rhythms for sound helps to engage an audience and establish an emotional context. Explore how you can convey different sounds with voice and body – eg *creaking door, wind, thunder, footsteps, applause, bird song, animal roaring and other sounds, traffic, splashing*.

- **The seven basic gestures** (See extract 14 on the accompanying DVD).

The seven basic gestures

Welcome
Palms outwards at waist height, bring them up and towards you in a welcoming gesture. Smiling, open face.

Love
Palms face inward, crossed on your chest. Head slightly inclined with soppy expression.

Think
Head leans on hand with forefinger against cheek. Thoughtful expression, furrowed brow.

Stop/no/no further
Hand palm out at almost shoulder height. Firm resolute expression. Can take one step forward at the same time.

Confused
Both hands, palm out, move at eye height as if finding way through bushes. Furrowed brow, worried expression.

Help
Palms up, hands move up and out as you look upwards with open mouth and appealing expression.

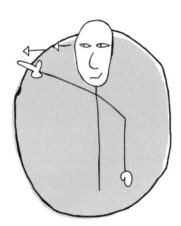

Look
Index finger moves outward at eye level, in the direction you want the audience to be looking. Concentrated, firm expression.

Our group found these extremely helpful, paired with voice. Once taught, they could use them in any story situation as appropriate.

You can find numerous other activities to develop gesture and mime in drama books, and on the Internet. See Section 8.

Note on gesture and sign

There is a distinct difference between sign language and gesture. Signs are actually the equivalent of words, and their use with speech is to convey or amplify the meaning of words. We found that if our group made too much use of sign, it was confusing rather than helpful. Try to encourage the use of large scale communicative basic gestures rather than too many signs. Some basic signs that are iconic (that is, they look like the concept they represent) can be useful, especially as starting points – eg *drink, eat, sleep, angry, no, go, come, give, love.*

5.4 **The language of story**

The language we use to tell a story consists of the choices we make in vocabulary and grammatical structure, use of poetic language and use of story specific words and phrases.

- **Vocabulary and grammar** – How rich and varied in choice of nouns, verbs, adjectives, adverbs; use of different verb tenses; use of complex clause structure and linking words such as *because, when, then, so, if.*

- **Poetic language** – Functions like music to give a pattern and rhythm, eg repetitions *(again and again)*; and employs figures of speech, such as metaphors, similes and well-known phrases or sayings.

- **Story-specific language** – Includes ways of starting and finishing stories, and words and phrases which go with particular stories.

Vocabulary and grammar

To extend the range of vocabulary you can take sets of characters, locations, weather, actions and brainstorm as many different words for describing them (adjectives and adverbs) and naming them (nouns and verbs) as you can. Make sure people use body language, facial expression and gesture as well (see *Voice the Word* on page 86). We were frankly astonished at the richness of language produced once we offered this simple stimulus. **(See extract 18 on the accompanying DVD.)**

We didn't concern ourselves too much about working on grammar and complex verb structures. These are probably the least important aspects of storytelling – many stories are told in the present tense, and the simpler the better. We did do specific work on linking events, using '*and then*'.

- **And then...** – One person begins and each person adds something to make a story, with *and then*... First this can be random, to encourage people to join in, but once people are familiar with this, each element needs to be related to the one before – show the link by joining people with a red wool connection.

Poetic language

We worked on speech rhythms and metaphor.

- **Speech rhythms** – Use of simple repetitive phrases, such as *on and on, again and again, further and further, or ever and ever.* Work on clapping or drum beats and helping people to talk or move to basic rhythms. You only need a few of these, employed regularly, to make telling effective.

- **Metaphor and simile** – As with language work, brainstorm some associations – *a giant is as tall as.....; her face was as white as ...; the hedge was as thick as...* Metaphors should be used sparingly, but can be applied from one story to another. Many metaphors are not used very originally, but are part of the fabric of stories (*yellow as gold, red as blood, blue as the sky*).

Story-specific language

As you research stories to tell, and listen to storytellers, collect examples of phrases that recur in tales. These function (just as they did for Homer in Ancient Greece) to buy time for the teller – they trip off the tongue and you don't have to think about them. Examples include 'further than far' for a journey; 'as kind as she was beautiful' for a heroine; 'nothing to eat but a crust of bread', and the type of metaphors listed above. Again, you only need a very few of these, and you will find that as you tell stories, people will begin to use this kind of language. The most useful repertoire is of phrases to start and finish stories, and to get audiences to respond (see below, Social aspects).

The other type of story-specific language is the recurrent rhymes and phrases that go with a particular story. You need to learn these like poetry. They can be put onto communication aids such as 'Big Macs' to help people join in. Examples include: *trip trap trip trap, over the rickety bridge* (Billy Goats Gruff); *Father Bear's was too ..., Mother Bear's was too... and Baby Bear's was just right* (Goldilocks and the Three Bears).

5.5 Social aspects of storytelling

The social aspects are all to do with awareness of the audience – introduction and closure of the story that makes reference to the audience; eye contact, feedback, incorporation of audience reactions and response to questions, listening, co-construction, awareness of needs of others.

Set up the space

Work with people to see how the space affects audience engagement. Experiment with different arrangements for chairs and benches – formal lines? Circle? Semicircle? How close? Take pictures and annotate these.

How to begin your story

Starters

- In a group, think of some ways of letting people know you have something to tell them: *listen to this, I've got something to tell you...something happened to me...you know what.... saying names with upward intonation...let me tell you... hey...I remember...*

- Traditional beginnings: *Once upon a time...long ago and far away...it is said that... Many years ago, in a time when memory was young... (India); A story, a story, let it come, let it go. (Traditional West African opening) Now here's a story I heard tell...*

Use call and response techniques.

This is a tradition which is very common in Africa – the teller calls a word or phrase, the audience responds and then the teller continues. Some traditional calls are these: crick/crack repeated three times (West Indies); see it, see it here/let it come for us to hear (Hausa); Bones, people/soup; Bones/meat; Bones/Bricks (Hungary and Central Europe).

Stop and listen!

Walk around the room to a beat. When it stops, touch the person nearest you on the arm, and say your opening sentence.

Hey you!

Get into groups. One group talks among themselves and the other group tries to attract their attention. Make a sound to start a story – clap hands, use a drum, bang foot on the floor, ring a bell.

Ritual

Brainstorm some rituals for letting the audience know that a story is about to begin. It could be the use of a rocking chair used only to tell stories in or a piece of cloth that comes out for story time. It could be a word or a phrase. Linda Goss, an African American teller shakes her rattle and calls out in a sing-song voice, 'story, storytelling time.'

Presence of the storyteller

It can be quite intimidating to come in and start telling stories. Examples of working directly on presence can be found in the introduction where the group work together **(See extract 1 on the accompanying DVD)** and the final sequence **(See extract 38 on the accompanying DVD)**, where people are working as individuals. You need to experiment with taking control of the storytelling space – find a position and a movement that you feel comfortable with. For example, walking slowly in, looking round, sitting down and putting your hands on your knees. Stand up and say 'I am a storyteller' – then take possession of the space.

- *Negative practice* – teachers/ trainers come and sit down in ways that do not give an audience confidence, eg too quick, head down, fiddling, sitting sideways on a chair, giggling, folding arms instead of open palm gesture on knees.

- *Position me* – following on from negative practice, students work to put the teacher/trainer in a better position, by physically moving her or him, or making suggestions.

Take digital photos of good and poor positioning, and get people to annotate the photos with comments.

Finishing

Sometimes it is really hard to finish a story and get off the stage!

Closing words – brainstorm and practise saying some phrases to end a story: *and that was it; that's the end; so we never went there again; there you go.*

Traditional endings – they lived happily ever after; that's all one, my story's done; My story is done. Let some go and let some come! (Ghana); And now the story is yours... My story is done/ But this story will go on, as long as grass grows and rivers run... (Native American); Now all is past: the story also, for all stories must come to an end at last .

Giving something to the audience – an object that is related to the story that you can throw for someone to catch or to pass round.

Actions to end your story – bowing to the audience, gesturing and clapping them to show that they were a good audience.

That's the end – As you go round the group, playing a game like 'I went shopping' one person is given a red card. When it is their turn, they make their contribution, then lay the card down, saying 'and that's the end'. They can then choose the next game.

That's the end (communal) – Tell and sign a traditional story all together (very short). At the end, everyone says, 'And that's the end' and drop their hands to their laps.

Let me know you're through – This game is based on some research done on Margaret Thatcher's interview style. She would routinely cue the interviewer that she had finished talking - dropping her voice at the end of a sentence, looking away, dropping her hands. Then when the hapless journalist tried to take his turn she would round on him saying, 'I haven't finished...' thus completely wrong-footing him. Decide beforehand what the end line of the story will be, and see how many cues you can give that you have finished. Count them or mark them on flip chart paper. Someone else then takes a turn.

I've started, you finish – In this game, one person starts a story and another person immediately finishes it. Can be done first in groups, together, then in teams, then in pairs, then with people jumping in.

Eye contact

Use the eye contact games listed in opening games to help people develop awareness of each other. Practise sweeping your gaze around the audience, just above their heads; including everyone in the audience; put the audience in a semicircle and make sure that the teller glances at everyone.

A good principle is that for description you look above the heads of the audience, whereas when addressing the audience or for dialogue, you look straight at them.

Negative practice

We found negative practice (ie doing things deliberately badly) was a stress free, fun way of learning what to do and what to avoid. We used it in many different situations, but it was particularly helpful for modelling good and poor social strategies, for both telling and listening. (See extracts 19–22 on the accompanying DVD.)

Audience participation

Listening to storytelling is never a passive activity. It helps to keep people engaged and understanding your stories if there are things they can do to join in. These could be:

- **Repetitions or predictable phrases** – eg *What are you doing? He walked on and on and on; I'm going to eat you up; Oh no you don't; we're going on a bear hunt; Little fish within the sea, remember the promise you made me.* The calls and responses used to open the story can be repeated during it to regain audience attention at transitional points.

- **Noises** – that are made within the tale: animal sounds, drum beats, marching with your feet, creaking doors, weather sounds.

- **Musical instruments** – but watch this, as you need to have absolute control.

- **Short songs or refrains** – *I'm a troll, fol de rol.*

- **Movements and gestures** – *they pulled and they pulled but they could not pull up the enormous turnip*; arms up in the air for a giant; side to side for being on a boat.

It is a good idea to teach these to your audience at the beginning of the storytelling session, so that they are prepared.

- **Asking questions** – at key points in the narrative you can stop and ask the audience what will happen next; why something has happened, what a character saw, smelt, felt, heard. These questions can be written on cards and shown to the audience if the teller is not confident enough to recall them verbally.

5.6 **Collaborative storytelling**

In our approach to storytelling, we emphasise collaboration and support. Try using the following steps to encourage students to work collaboratively on the story.

Here is a story which needs to be told. The question is NOT how much of it you can remember, but what it means to you, why you enjoy it, and what you will be contributing to it. Your partner(s) are there to support you in the telling, and help you enjoy it.

- Ensure that students can make eye contact and touch or share objects. Your position should be behind or at the back, between them, so that you can facilitate their interaction, and direct them to the audience.

- Ask the storyteller to start the story off and say as much as they can about their own story. Then ask their companion to chip in anything else. Then you can show them pictures and use the puppets to remember the story sequence.

- Talk together about what the storyteller and the companion teller are good at – which is their favourite bit of the story, and what is most effective in their telling. Help them to decide which bits of the story they are responsible for. Record this on a form.

- Think about music and gestures that you can all use in the telling and how you are going to use them.

- Tell the story together. The role of the facilitator is to prompt when necessary, possibly by taking on some of the narrative thread. **(See extracts 6 and 34 on the accompanying DVD.)**

Learning to tell

Section 6:
Example stories

In this section you will find some examples of stories to use with the group (the story themes). A suggested format is:

- in the **first term** you might work with stories about beginnings – creation myths and where stories come from

- in the **second term** you could move on to stories about identity and belonging

- in the **final term** tackle something like a hero cycle, where people are developing real confidence and style as storytellers

Mixed in with these themes you can use some seasonal stories. We suggest ending the year with retelling a story like the story stone (how stories came into the world) which leaves people with the responsibility of going out into the world to tell stories.

6.1 **Creation stories**

Maheo makes the world
(Native American: Cheyenne)

In the beginning, there was no world, nothing. Shut your eyes and imagine it. Put your hands over your ears and listen. Nothing to see, nothing to hear.

Maheo, the Great Spirit who lived in the nothing, was lonely, and he began to cry. And from his tears there came a great stretch of salt water. And Maheo spoke and created fishes to swim under the water, and birds to fly in the air above the water. And for a time the fishes splashed and the birds sang and all were content. But then the birds came to Maheo and said that they were tired of flying and that they needed somewhere to rest. And Maheo said, 'I can do this, but I need your help to find a small piece of mud and then I can make you a world to rest in'. And the eagle said, 'I will try'. And he flew as high as the sun, and he dived as deep as the shadows, but he came back with nothing. And all the birds tried in their turn, but none could fine the mud that would make the world. And then the smallest bird of all, the little coot, asked if she might try. And Maheo said, 'Go with my blessing'. And the little coot dived down and swam away for a very long time. And finally she came back, and she swam up to the hands of Maheo, and into his hands she dropped a tiny, tiny piece of mud. From that mud, Maheo made the world, and on the world he put trees for the birds to rest in.

(Adapted from a version in *Earthtales*, by Alida Gersie).

Discussion points

A group is a bit like a world. We are at the beginning of our group. What does the story tell us? (that everyone has a role to play, that we should listen even to the smallest, quietest person). Your discussion about hopes and fears and rules can come from this story.

Activity

Make some figures out of clay and display them. Use these later to build stories.

How stories came into the world
(Native American: Seneca told by Henry Jacob)

At first in the world, no-one knew what a story was. There was once a little boy who was a fine hunter. He used to go every day to the forest to hunt. One day he went deeper into the woods than ever in search of birds to shoot. At midday he wanted to sit down to have his lunch. He spotted a lake and in the middle of it, a high, smooth, flat-topped, round stone. He went to the stone, sprang up on to it and sat down. He was about to eat his dinner when he heard a voice saying, 'Shall I tell you stories?' The boy looked round but could see no-one. Again he raised the food to his mouth, and again he heard the voice. It came from the stone on which he was sitting. He was very surprised, but he asked, 'What is that? What does it mean to tell stories?'

'It is telling what happened a long time ago. If you will give me your birds, I'll tell you stories.'

'You may have the birds.'

As soon as the boy promised to give the birds, the stone began telling what happened long ago. When one story was told, another was begun. The boy sat, with his head down, and listened. Towards night the stone said, 'We will rest now. Come again tomorrow.'

When he got home, his family asked why there were no birds for dinner. The boy said that game was scarce and he had not found any. The next morning he set off again, but he forgot to hunt for birds, he was thinking of the stories the stone had told him. When a bird lighted near him he shot it, but he kept straight on toward the opening in the woods. When he got there he put his birds on the stone, and called out, 'I've come! Here are birds. Now tell me stories.'

The stone told story after story. Toward night it said, 'Now we must rest till tomorrow.'

On the way home the boy looked for birds, but it was late and he found only a few. The boy's family wondered why he was no longer bringing home so much food. So they followed him the next day. They too listened to the stories told by the stone. When it was almost night the stone said, 'Tomorrow all the people in your village must come and listen to my stories. Tell the chief to send every man, and have each man bring something to eat. You must clean the brush away so the people can sit on the ground near me.'

Continued

That night Poyeshaon told the chief about the story-telling stone, and gave him the stone's message. The chief sent a runner to give the message to each family in the village. Early the next morning everyone in the village was ready to start. Poyeshaon went ahead and the crowd followed. When they came to the opening each man put what he had brought, meat or bread, on the stone; the brush was cleared away, and every one sat down.

When all was quiet the stone said, 'Now I will tell you stories of what happened long ago. There was a world before this. The things that I am going to tell about happened in that world. Some of you will remember every word that I say, some will remember a part of the words, and some will forget them all, I think this will be the way, but each man must do the best he can. Hereafter, you must tell these stories to one another, now listen.'

Every day the stone told stories until one day it gave a great heave and said, 'I have finished! You must keep these stories as long as the world lasts; tell them to your children and grandchildren generation after generation. One person will remember them better than another. When you go to a man or a woman to ask for one of these stories carry something to pay for it, bread or meat, or whatever you have. I know all that happened in the world before this; I have told it to you. When you visit one another, you must tell these things, and keep them up always. I have finished.' And the stone split into many pieces and each person took a piece away.

And so it has been. From the stone came all the knowledge the Senecas have of the world before this.

(Adapted from: www.firstpeople.us/FP-Html-Legends/The-Origin-Of-Stories-Seneca.html).

Discussion points

This is a perfect starting point for discussion of what makes a story and the story structure activities.

Activity

Have enough stones for everyone in the room. Or have a sheet with pieces of rock drawn on them. Each person must write the name of a story they know in the rocks on the sheet. People can write the name of their favourite story that they would like to practise telling, on the pebble. An obvious starter game is 'pass the pebble'.

The bag of stories
(Korean)

There was once a boy called Dong Chin who loved stories. But he wanted to keep them all to himself. So he put every story he heard into a bag and hung it up by the door. He would take one out every night, and listen to his favourites, and push and push a new one inside. He never ever shared these stories, and so once they were in the bag, there they stayed – and no-one else ever heard them either. When he grew up, the bag was full of stories – so full that all the story spirits inside were squashed and uncomfortable. Now the young man was going to get married, and the night before the wedding, his faithful servant was making sure everything was ready. It took a long time, and it was midnight before he sat down on the verandah. Dong Chin himself was fast asleep and snoring. Suddenly he heard some low voices talking and rustling, coming from the bag.

'I can't bear it any more.'

'We've got to do something.'

'He's getting married – we'll have our revenge!'

'We need to punish him for keeping us in this bag for years.'

'I'm a story about a poisoned well. With my magic powers I shall send it to the side of the road. When he drinks from it, he will get really ill.'

'Great idea,' said another. 'I'm a story with poisoned berries in it. I'll put them further down the road so if he doesn't drink from the well, he will eat them and get ill.'

'Right,' said still another. 'I'm a story with a big snake. I'll put it under the bed that he comes to with his new wife, and when they are asleep it will slip out and bite them so they die.'

The servant was determined to help. So the following day when the wedding party set out, he went in front, leading the horse. It was a very hot day, and soon Dong Chin was thirsty. Just then he saw a well of beautiful clear water, sparkling in the sunshine. 'Servant,' he cried, 'bring me a drink.'

'Oh no,' said the servant, 'certainly not'. And he hurried past the well.

Continued

Dong Chin was very surprised and cross, but it was too late. Suddenly he saw some beautiful red berries growing on a bush. 'I would like some of those,' he said, 'get them for me.'

'Oh no,' said the servant, 'certainly not.' And he hurried past the bush.

Dong Chin was really cross now. 'What do you think you are doing?' he shouted. 'You are my servant and you should obey me.'

'Trust me, young master' said the servant.

They arrived at the bride's house. She was very beautiful, and everyone was happy. The young couple were married and there was a wonderful party. When night fell they went to their bedroom, and knelt down to say their prayers. They looked into each other's eyes. What a tender moment it was! But suddenly there was a great bang and the door flew open. In rushed the servant carrying a huge kitchen knife. The bride screamed, and Dong Chin shouted. 'Look out,' called the servant, and out came a huge snake.

The servant raised the knife high above his head and brought it down, CHOP on the snake's head. They were saved. Now the servant could explain his strange behaviour. He told them all about the story spirits.

Dong Chin realized how badly he had treated the stories all his life. 'I promise,' he said, 'that from now on I will share all the stories and let them go free into the world'. And he did.

(Adapted from: www.aaronshep.com/stories/o6o.html).

Discussion points

The message here is that stories need to be heard and told. We have a responsibility to pass stories on. Perhaps it also tells us about what might happen if we bottle up the experiences that happen to us, and don't have a chance to tell them to other people.

Activity

Make your own story bag and fill it with the stories you know, or different types of story.

6.2 **Origin stories**

Coyote steals fire (Native American: Crow)

Long ago, man lived in the world, and it was summer. But then autumn came and the leaves dropped from the trees and the wind blew. And then winter came with the snow, and it was cold, so cold. And man was afraid for the children and the old people as they shivered through the day and night. Coyote did not fear the winter, because of his warm fur, but he felt sorry for the men and women.

He knew of a faraway mountain top where three Fire Beings lived. They had fire to keep people warm, but they would not let anyone come near. Coyote decided to get the fire to help men and women. He asked the other animals to help him, and told them to wait along the track that led up the mountain. He crept up close to the top. There was the fire, and there were the terrible Fire Beings, with their burning eyes, their sharp teeth and fingers like claws. They heard Coyote slip on a stone, and they looked round, but could see nothing. Coyote crept closer. He brushed against a tree, and the Fire Beings leapt up at the sound. But they could see nothing. Coyote watched the Fire Beings tend the fire and learned what to do. When dawn came, the Fire Beings went to sleep. Coyote crept closer and closer and then he leapt at the fire and seized a burning branch in his mouth. He raced as fast as he could down the hill. Immediately the Fire Beings awoke, and screamed in fury. They flew after him, faster than the eye could see. One of them reached out and touched his tail – which turned white as she did so, and it is white to this day. Coyote flung the fire to the first animal, who was Squirrel. It burned a long dark stripe along her back as she swung through the trees. As the Fire Beings caught up with her, she flung it to Frog, who caught it in his mouth and hopped away. The Fire Beings lunged at Frog and grabbed his tail, but Frog gave a great jump and left his tail behind in their hands – that's why Frogs have no tail. Frog threw the fire brand to Tree, and Tree swallowed it.

The Fire Beings came to Tree and asked for their fire back. But Tree stood firm. Even when they cut him and shouted at him, he kept it. So the Fire Beings went back to the mountain. But Coyote knew how to get fire from the Tree. He showed men and women how to rub two sticks together. And so they gained Fire. And the fire that stayed in the heart of the Tree turned to coal – and we heat our homes with it to this day. Thanks to Coyote we are warm in winter.

(Adapted from a version in *Earthtales*, by Alida Gersie).

Discussion

This story tells us about fire. Fire is a good way of thinking about the energy and power inside us that help us to work, to create, and to be full of life. Imagine the fire inside you and see if you can make a gesture or a picture to show it working.

The animals had to help each other to get the fire. Can you think of who helps you, and how they do it? And how do you help other people?

Activity

Make a ball of fire with tissue paper in red, orange, pink and gold. Throw it between you. Keep it to remind yourselves of the fire at the heart of the stories you tell.

How the birds got their colours

Right at the beginning of time, when God was sorting out the order and hierarchy of all the things below the firmament, He created the birds, and then finally got round to giving them their colours later when most other things had been done. 'Gather round, birds,' he commanded.

The sky was filled with a gigantic sound of rustling feathers as a thousand wings flapped – so many birds that they almost put out the Sun! There was a terrible squawking and squabbling as the birds pushed each other to be first in the queue for God's paintbrush.

'Come and form an orderly queue,' said God. 'My paintbox is overflowing with all the beautiful colours – plenty to go around.'

First came the SWAN. Serene, silent and beautiful, gliding on the waters of dawn, God gave the swan feathers of the purest white.

Next, the RAVEN of the crags and mountain tops. Bird of doom and winter, said God, and painted the raven as black as a November night. 'Krok' said the raven.

Next came (any other birds you want to name). At last the paint box was empty. But right at the end of the queue was the smallest, dullest, brownest, tiniest little bird.

'You're too late,' said God.

'I'm sorry,' said the LARK. 'I had to be up so early, I had an afternoon nap – missed all the fun...'

Continued

'Come here,' said God, and whispered in the lark's ear. 'My colours are all gone, except for the smallest piece of gold. Too small to make much difference. But close your eyes and open your mouth.'

He popped the last little bit of gold into the lark's throat. And that's why the lark has the sweetest song of all.

Listen.
(Play a tune on the flute or a CD of The Lark Ascending by Ralph Vaughan Williams).

(From a version told by Jem Dick).

Discussion

What makes us unique? What are our favourite colours, activities? What can we learn about each other? The story also says we should not judge by appearances. What are your hidden talents? This story goes well with the identity activities from the list of warm-up games.

Why the jackal has a stripe on his back
(South Africa: collected by James Honey, 1910)

The Sun, it is said, was one day on Earth, and the men who were travelling saw him sitting by the wayside, but passed him without notice. Jackal, however, who came after them, and also sitting, went to him and said, 'Such a fine little child is left behind by the men.' He then took Sun up, and put it into his awa-skin (on his back). When it burnt him, he said, 'Get down,' and shook himself; but Sun stuck fast to his back, and burnt Jackal's back black from that day.

(Adapted from: www.sacred-texts.com/afr/saft/sft40.htm).

Why the zebra has stripes
(Africa: San, Namibia)

Long, long ago, at the beginning of time, the land was dry and there was no water except in a few holes in the earth. A baboon (monkey, show picture) claimed that one of the waterholes belonged only to him. He would not let anyone come near, and he built a fire to keep people away. A zebra came by. He had travelled a long way and was tired and thirsty. In those days, the zebra was just white. He had no stripes at all. He asked if he could drink from the water hole, but the baboon jumped up and down and shouted 'No, no, no, go away'. They argued and got into a fight. The zebra kicked the baboon so hard that the baboon flew up in the air, and the zebra fell backwards into the fire. When he got up, he had stripes all over his back from the charcoal sticks – and the baboon had a red bottom from the zebra's kick. That's how they have been ever since!

(Adapted from: www.felid.org/activities/page_97.htm).

The legend of the robin's red breast
(Traditional English)

A little brown bird shared Bethlehem's stable with the holy family. One night, as the family lay sleeping, she noticed their fire was going out. So she flew down from the rafters and fanned the fire with her wings throughout the night in order to keep the baby Jesus warm. In the morning, she was rewarded with a red breast as a symbol of her love for the newborn king.

See also all the *Just So stories* by Rudyard Kipling.

Discussion

These stories are told to explain why people, animals and nature are the way they are. They have other lessons to tell us – about the consequences of what we do. Lots of discussion here about what makes us the way we are, and could we be any different. Links well with the identity collage activity.

Activity

Think of animals or natural characteristics and brainstorm some story ideas for why they are that way.

6.3 Seasonal stories

Persephone – spring and autumn
(Ancient Greece)

Persephone was the young daughter of the Earth goddess, Demeter. She brought all the spring flowers with her. One day as she was out in the fields, the dark God of the Underworld, Hades, saw her. He kidnapped her and took her below ground to live with him. Demeter called and called for her daughter, but no-one could tell her what had happened. She searched all over the world for her, and forgot to look after the earth. So the leaves withered and fell, and the Sun went in, and the plants died and the Earth shivered. The great God Zeus saw what was happening, and told Demeter that she could have her daughter back – as long as she had eaten nothing in the underworld. He sent his messenger, Hermes, to fetch her. But Persephone had eaten something – six pomegranate seeds. So Zeus decreed that she must stay with Hades for six months of each year. So now, when she returns to Earth, spring and summer come and Demeter rejoices to have her daughter back again. But every autumn and winter the goddess of spring goes underground.

Discussion

This is a story about loss and grief, but also renewal. People may find themselves talking about people who have died or who they do not see any more. It also tells us that we sometimes make choices that really affect what happens to us – and then we have to take the consequences.

Activity

Make a collage of autumn, winter and spring while listening to music.

Diwali – festival of lights
(Hindu, India)

Lord Rama and his wife Sita and his brother Lakshmana were exiled to the forest. The wicked demon Ravana saw Sita and fell in love with her. He sent a magic white deer to trick Rama and Lakshmana, who chased it through the forest, leaving Sita alone. Ravan captured Sita and took her to his island fortress. But the Monkey King Hanuman told Rama what had happened, and they fought a great battle to get Sita back. Then Rama, Sita and Lakshmana returned to their city, and people lit divas (little candles) to light their way.

Discussion

Think about what Ravana represents (evil, greed) and the other characters. Central to Hindu philosophy is the assertion that there is something beyond the physical body and mind which is pure, infinite, and eternal, called the Atman. Diwali celebrates the Inner Light, and the dispelling of ignorance and darkness.

Activity

Make divas out of clay and rangouli patterns (traditionally drawn with the fingers using flour, rice grains or coloured chalk). Create a path or labyrinth lit by the divas that you walk round.

Baboushka
(Traditional Russian)

There was once an old woman called Baboushka, who was very proud of her house. She always did lots and lots of housework. One snowy night, there was a knock on her door. She was amazed when she opened it to find three kings there, with their servants and their treasures. They asked for a bed for the night, and of course she agreed. She asked where they were going, and they told her that they were seeking the baby Jesus. In the morning, they invited her to go with them. Babushka said she would love to – but she had to clear up the house first. She spent a long time making everything clean and neat, and then she got together a basket of toys for the baby. By the time she got to the stable, the Holy Family had gone. So now she travels the world, giving her toys to children at Christmas, because any one of them might be the Christ child.

Discussion

What does this story tell us about making choices – do we sometimes have to take risks? What memories of gifts do you have? Do you know any babies – what gifts are good for them?

Activity

Prepare your own basket of pretend Christmas gifts (which can be given to people as a closing activity). Draw or write on paper.

Chinese New Year

There are several legends about how the animals were chosen for the Chinese zodiac (rat, ox, tiger, rabbit, dragon, snake, horse, sheep, monkey, rooster, dog, and boar). This is one of them. The Jade Emperor is the name of the Emperor of Heaven.

Long ago, in China, the Jade Emperor decided there should be a way of measuring time. On his birthday he told the animals that there was to be a swimming race. The first twelve animals across the fast flowing river would be the winners and they would each have a year of the zodiac named after them.

All the animals lined up along the river bank. The rat and the cat, who were good friends, were worried because they were poor swimmers. Being clever they asked the strong ox if he would carry them across the river.

'Of course,' said the kind ox. 'Just climb on my back and I will take you across.'

The rat and the cat quickly jumped up and were very excited when the ox soon took the lead in the race. They had almost reached the other bank when the rat pushed the cat into the river leaving him to struggle in the water. Then just before the ox was about to win the race the rat leapt on his head and on to the bank to win the race.

'Well done,' said the Jade Emperor to the proud rat. 'The first year of the zodiac will be named after you.'

The poor ox had been tricked into second place and the second year of the zodiac was named after him. Shortly after the exhausted tiger clawed his way to the river bank to claim third place. Swimming across the river had been an enormous struggle for him against the strong currents. The Emperor was so delighted with his efforts that he named the third year after him. The next animals to come were the rabbit (fourth), who had not swum at all, but jumped across stepping stones and logs. The dragon was next, and the Emperor asked him why he had taken so long, when he was so good at flying and swimming.

'I was held up because some people and animals needed water to drink. I needed to make some rain,' the dragon explained. 'Then when I was nearly here I saw a poor little rabbit on a log in the water and I blew a puff of wind so that the log would float to the river bank.'

Continued

'Well that was very kind of you and now you are here you will have the fifth year of the zodiac named after you.'

The horse came next, but the snake twined himself around the horse's hooves, tripped him up and got into sixth place, so the horse was the seventh year. Not long afterwards a raft arrived carrying the goat, the monkey and the rooster. They explained to the Emperor how they had shared the raft that the rooster had found. The goat and monkey had cleared weeds and pushed the raft to the shore. The Emperor was very pleased that the animals had worked together. He said the goat would be the eighth zodiac animal, the monkey the ninth and the rooster the tenth. The next animal to finish was the dog.

'Why are you so late when you are one of the best swimmers?' asked the Jade Emperor.

'The water in the river was so clean that I had to have a bath on the way,' explained the dog.

His reward was to have the eleventh year named after him.

Now there was one place left in the zodiac and the Emperor wondered when the last winner would come. He had nearly given up when he heard a grunt from the boar.

'You took a long time to cross the river,' said the Emperor to the boar.

'I was hungry and stopped to eat,' explained the boar. 'After the meal I felt so tired that I fell asleep.'

'You have still done well,' said the Jade Emperor. 'The last year of the zodiac will be named after you.'

As for the cat who had been pushed into the water by the rat, he finally crawled out of the water, but was too late to have a year named after him. He felt very cross with the rat and since then cats have never been friends with rats. From that day to this the Chinese zodiac has followed this cycle of years named after these twelve animals.

Discussion

What does this story tell us about the ways in which people behave? If you had been the Jade Emperor, what would you have said to the animals?

Activity

Find out your own animal and horoscope. Group with others who are the same as you. Talk about whether you are like your animal sign. Act your animal sign for others to guess.

6.4 Hero cycle: Tales of King Arthur

The aim of these stories is to develop a set of personal narratives linked to life history, within the context of the Arthurian legend

Theme 1 – **The childhood of Arthur: taken from parents, fostered with Sir Ector, loses touch with his sister; bullied by Kay**
Your memories: of childhood; best memories of family; separating from the family; disinheritance, bullying; life growing up away from the city – on the farm. Good memories: Christmas, birthdays, holiday.

Theme 2 – **Sword in the stone: how King Arthur found the sword Excalibur and founded the Round Table**
Mentors at school, who were your teachers, wise people in your community; church, grandfather, mentor, appoint your guardian.
Who were the people who said – you can't do that; failures at school.
What are your achievements – what are you proud of?

Theme 3 – **The coming together of the Round Table – fellowship and friendship: stories of Sir Gawain**
Who were your friends, and what do you remember about them? Shared goals. Concept of a company – supertop trumps – your strength and your weakness. The tasks for the Round Table: slay dragons; protect the weak, quest, learn skills. What challenges and problems have you faced – when have you behaved bravely like a hero?

Theme 4 – **Quest for the Holy Grail. What do you put into the grail, what do you take from it, where will you find it?**
The grail quest relates to our own aspirations for our lives – the treasure we would like to find, the aims we want to fulfil.

Theme 5 – **The end of the Round Table – death of Arthur, the Once and Future King.**
Dealing with endings and new beginnings – what we have lost and feel sad about, but good memories to keep. The Knights of the Round Table lost their King, but went on to other things. When King Arthur comes back, what will he ask of you, his knights? What will you tell him of your achievements?

Section 7:
What's on the DVD and how to use it

7.1 Introduction to the DVD

The DVD that accompanies this book contains further material to illustrate and reinforce the text:

- **Video footage** of Openstorytellers' inclusive storytelling sessions, demonstrating a range of storytelling, games and activities

- **Links to the two organisations**:

  - Openstorytellers

    - Find out more about this unique group of community storytellers who have learning disabilities

    - Find out about OCN accreditation

  - British Institute of Learning Disabilities
    Find out more about BILD's work with and for people with a learning disability

- **Forms and information sheets**
  Section 9 of this handbook contains appendices. These forms and information sheets have also been saved on the DVD as PDF files so you can print off as many copies as you need of each appendix, or include them as an attachment to an e-mail. Simply click on the form you want to download

7.2 **How to use the DVD**

When you insert the DVD into your computer drive, a screen should open in your usual browser window, similar to that below. This is the *Learning to tell* Home page.

Learning to tell Home page

If the screen doesn't automatically appear when you insert the disk, simply click on the 'index.htm' icon within the containing folder of the DVD (Go to 'My Computer' > 'Devices with Removable Storage' > 'Learning to tell (D)').

Playing the video clips

At various places throughout the handbook, the text refers to a relevant video clip, and an icon to the right of the page provides a quick summary of which video clips it would be helpful to watch, example below.

Portfolios

Portfolios are the cumulative records of stories collected over time. The DVD that accompanies this book offers an example of a portfolio with both personal and traditional stories. (See extract 7 on the accompanying DVD.)

To watch the video clip, click on the 'View the *Learning to tell* video clips' link on the left of the opening screen of the DVD shown above. This will take you to a screen from where you can view all the video clips individually in any order you please.

Video clip introductory screen

The introductory screen for the video clips features numbered links (1 – 38) at the bottom of the screen. Each number is a link to the relevant video extract. By rolling your cursor over each number, you can see the title of each clip appearing directly above the numbers. Simply click on the number of the video extract you want to watch.

A full list of the video extracts and a brief description of each can be found on pages 121–124 of this handbook.

On every screen, in the top right-hand corner are 'Exit' and 'Help' buttons. By clicking on the EXIT button ⓧ you will quit out of the video extract and return to the *Learning to tell* Home page from where you can follow other links. By clicking on the HELP button ⑦ a PDF file will open automatically, with instructions on how to use the DVD. Both buttons can be accessed from all screens.

Video extract screen

The STOP and PLAY/PAUSE buttons

When you select a video extract, the clip will start to play automatically. A PAUSE button ⏸ allows you to pause the video at any point and this toggles with a PLAY button ▷ so you can resume playing the clip. By moving the vertical bar of the progress bar you can fast forward or rewind the clip to any point. If you click on the STOP button ☐ the video clip will return to the beginning.

Links to the two organisations behind *Learning to tell*

Learning to tell Home page

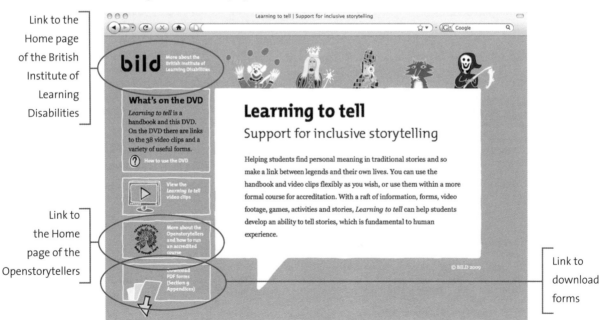

Link to the Home page of the British Institute of Learning Disabilities

Link to the Home page of the Openstorytellers

Link to download forms

Openstorytellers

Openstorytellers is a unique group of community storytellers who have learning disabilities. By visiting their website, www.openstorytellers.org.uk, you can find out a little more about their vision and how they began, meet the people involved, read about their performances and training, gain an understanding of the way the group works and obtain contact details.

You can integrate the *Learning to tell* materials into a more formal course for accreditation on the Open College Network course *Inclusive Storytelling*. The Openstorytellers website also contains information about OCN accreditation.

British Institute of Learning Disabilities

The British Institute of Learning Disabilities (BILD) is committed to improving the quality of life for people with a learning disability by involving them and their families in all aspects of their work. You can find out about how they work with the government and public bodies to achieve full citizenship, how they undertake beneficial research and development projects and how they work with service providers to develop and share good practice.

Forms and information sheets

Section 9 of this handbook (page 129) contains appendices. Copies of these forms and information sheets have also been saved on the DVD as PDF files so that you can print off as many copies as you need of each appendix, or include them as an attachment to an e-mail.

Select the 'Download PDF forms' link at the botttom left of the *Learning to tell* Home page. This will take you to the Download Appendices page.

Download Appendices page

Simply double click on the image of the appendix page that you need. This will download it as a PDF file.

Find the appendix that you need and simply click on either the image or the title. This will download a PDF file of the page(s). You may want to specify a folder where the file will be saved. You can then either print it or attach it to an e-mail in the usual way.

7.3 The video clips

Extract 1   **The Unlimited Company introduce themselves**
This introduction is also an example of a group working together to take control of the space and introduce themselves to the audience. Note how people are sitting, speaking, eye contact – and also anything that might be improved.

Extract 2   ***Story theme:* Loss, disability, rebirth**
Performance of *Ceridwen's Cauldron*
This footage is provided to show the group telling the story – we had completed one year of the inclusive storytelling programme, but had limited rehearsal time.

Extract 3   ***Story theme:* Discussion**
This is an example of reflection on the personal relevance and meaning of the story.

Extract 4   ***Story lines 1:* Life story**
Here one person tells a life story – an example of a 'big' story as it has profound meaning for him. Consider what the links might be between the traditional and the personal story. The big life story is contrasted with the amusing personal anecdote (see 6, below) which does not have the same resonance, though it is also very significant.

Extract 5   ***Story lines 2:* Personal photos**
This is the very beginning of developing story lines. Think about the difference between the narrated stories and the simple basic naming of photographs that is going on here. There is the germ of a story when she talks about the boat which was not working properly. We might choose to develop this into a more extended narrative together.

Extract 6   ***Story lines 3:* Personal anecdote**
This lovely story shows how when you have a good story that you are motivated to tell, you can really communicate! Stories like these become part of the group memory, for retrieving and laughing about together. In that sense, as well as a story line, this contributes to story company. Notice the roles that people are taking to support the teller where necessary.

| *Extract 7* | **Story lines 4: Portfolio examples** |
| | Some examples of the portfolio, moving between traditional (the pumpkin tale and the witch) and personal stories. The portfolio is made up of drawings, photographs and writing. |

| *Extract 8* | **Story skills: Structural 1 – Memory game** |
| | This is a safari game, where each player turns over a card, names an animal, suggests how it contributes to the story and finally has to recall all the animals that have preceded it. The main emphasis is memory and linking. |

| *Extract 9* | **Story skills: Structural 2 – Story components** |
| | An example of a story cube – first played very simply, then with some elaboration. |

| *Extract 10* | **Story skills: Structural 3 – Characters** |
| | This extended discussion starts with identifying the characters, drawn as puppets. |

| *Extract 11* | **Story skills: Structural 4 – Sequencing** |
| | Then moves onto problem solving about how to use the puppets as cues for the sequence of the story, which could easily be muddled. By leaving space for people to come up with solutions, creative thinking is enhanced. |

| *Extract 12* | **Story skills: Structural 5 – Storytelling with the Khavad** |
| | We included this piece of narrative to show how the Khavad works. Note that the teller does not allow himself to be distracted by the complexity of managing the resource. |

| *Extract 13* | **Story skills: Feelings 1 – Facial expressions** |
| | An example of a copycat game, which is actually quite hard to play. |

| *Extract 14* | **Story skills: Feelings 2 – Gestures** |
| | Together the group try to remember the seven basic gestures, which sometimes come out as eight or nine. |

| *Extract 15* | **Story skills: Feelings 3 – Voice** |
| | In this team activity we use planning and guessing as strategies for working on ways to change intonation, pitch, volume of voice, here at the level of a sentence. |

| *Extract 16* | **Story skills: Feelings 4 – Voice and gesture** |
| | An example of building progression and climax through varying speed and volume, this time with one word. |

Extract 17 **Story skills: *Feelings 5* – Putting it together**
This extract illustrates how we then try to apply what we have been practising in the games in the real context of telling the story.

Extract 18 **Story skills: Language description**
Drawing is a very good stimulus for language work – it takes the pressure off memory and gives you something to focus on while you think. Working in a group also allows people to bounce ideas off each other.

Extract 19 **Story skills: *Social 1* – Bad telling**
Probably our favourite activity. Spot the mistakes.

Extract 20 **Story skills: *Social 2* – Good telling**
And the corrections.

Extract 21 **Story skills: *Social 3* – Bad listening**
And again.

Extract 22 **Story skills: *Social 4* – Good listening**
Some examples here of positive feedback by the group.

Extract 23 **Story company 1 Physical warm-ups**
Here members of the group have learned to take responsibility for leading simple exercises.

Extract 24 **Story company 2 Voice warm-ups**
This work on voice leads directly into some of the activities using voice listed previously.

Extract 25 **Story company 3 Opening games – Minestrone**
These games show that warm-ups can involve both verbal and non-verbal skills. Before the debrief, list the skills that each game is developing.

Extract 26 **Story company 4 Opening games – Pass the clap**

Extract 27 **Story company 5 Opening games – Pass the touch**

Extract 28 **Story company 6 News introduction**
It's important to make it clear why each activity is undertaken, as the leader does here in explaining the news group.

Extract 29   **Story company 7** **News small group**
Here the leader tells his news, hands over to another person, checks that she has finished and starts the next person off. There are some nice responses to each other – no trainers were present.

Extract 30   **Story company 8** **News feedback**
The leader economically conveys the most important pieces of news – if he gets it wrong no-one minds and they can chip in.

Extract 31   **Story company 9** **Group support strategies**
The group are thinking back not only to how they welcomed new people, but how they felt when they started.

Extract 32   **Story company 10** **Group problem solving**
Trying to stop people who go on and on is one of the most difficult issues to face. We haven't always cracked it, but this extract shows how useful it is to put the problem to the group, in the context where rules have been clearly agreed.

Extract 33   **Story company 11** **Group rules**
Here we remembered some of the rules we developed at the beginning of the inclusive storytelling programme. In the first weeks, we went through them explicitly each week.

Extract 34   **Story company 12** **Shared memories at lunchtime**
Informal storytelling really supports the more formal work. The shared memories, good and bad, are what build a strong group identity.

Extract 35   **Story company 13** **Symbolic ritual**
The special chair is marked out with a piece of cloth and is left in the circle only at the beginning and end of the day.

Extract 36   **Story company 14** **Feedback circle**
In the feedback we focus on what happened during the actual day, gently reminding people who stray beyond this remit. People are encouraged to say anything they did not like so well or would change next time.

Extract 37   **Story company 15** **Closing game**
The closing activity functions like a letting go or relaxation.

Extract 38   **I am a storyteller**
Another example of the social skill of taking control of the story space, reinforced by negative practice, explicit modelling, feedback and looking at oneself on camera.

Section 8:
Resources

Organisations

Derbyshire Language Scheme

www.derbyshire-language-scheme.co.uk

Emerson College
Forest Row
E Sussex RH18 5JX

Tel: 0044 (0)1342 822238

www.emerson.org.uk

International centre for adult education based on the work of Rudolf Steiner. Runs several storytelling courses.

George Ewart Evans Centre for Storytelling
Cardiff School of Creative & Cultural Industries
ATRiuM
University of Glamorgan
Adam Street
Cardiff CF24 2XF

Tel: 0044 (0)1443 668631

storytelling.research.glam.ac.uk
www.storyworksglam.co.uk

Based at the University of Glamorgan, the centre is dedicated to promoting, teaching, developing and researching storytelling in all its forms. It runs courses and conferences.

Society for Storytelling
Morgan Library
Aston Street
Wem SY4 5AU

Tel: 0044(0)7534 578386

www.sfs.org.uk

The Society for Storytelling offers events, a magazine and website. The Society welcomes anyone with an interest in oral storytelling, whether teller, listener, beginner or professional.

Scottish Storytelling Centre
43–45 High Street
Edinburgh EH1 1SR

Tel: 0044 (0)131 556 9579

www.scottishstorytellingcentre.co.uk

Supports a national network of storytellers involved in outreach projects with local authorities, environmental agencies, community centres and libraries, engaging with all age groups and diverse cultures of modern Scotland.

The Story Museum
Rochester House
42 Pembroke Street
Oxford OX1 1BP

www.storymuseum.org.uk

Centre for children's literature and storytelling.

Websites

Storytelling in Ireland

www.storytellersofireland.org

Story collections

www.livingmyths.com/Celticyear.htm
(For more information on legends)

www.mythstories.com
 (A web-based museum of myth and fable)

www.healingstory.org
(For stories to address health and difficult situations)

www.story-lovers.com

www.storynet.org

www.timsheppard.co.uk/story

www.creativekeys.net/StorytellingPower/article1020.html

www.derekburrows.com/storytelling%20tips-details.pdf

www.aaronshep.com/stories/o60.html
(This site contains a fuller version of 'The bag of stories' from Korea)

www.firstpeople.us/FP-Html-Legends/The-Origin-Of-Stories-Seneca.html
(This site contains a fuller version of 'How stories came into the world')

www.sacred-texts.com/afr/saft/sft40.htm
(This site contains the story: 'Why the jackal has a stripe on his back')

www.felid.org/activities/page_97.htm
(This site contains the story: 'Why the zebra has stripes')

www.ilhawaii.net/~stony/loreindx.html
(This site offers a fuller version of 'Coyote Steals Fire')

www.folktale.net

Personal communication passports

www.communicationpassports.org.uk/Home/index.php

Voice work

www.ncvs.org/e-learning/warmup.html

www.santarosa.edu/~gbegin/right.html

Name games

www.svlinc.com/Public/shared/crowdbreaker_namegames1.htm

www.wilderdom.com/games/

www.residentassistant.com/games/namegames.htm

Gesture and mime

www.shambles.net/pages/learning/performing/dramagame/

www.dramaresource.com/

Communication aids

www.communicationmatters.org.uk

Traditional story openings

www.folktale.net/openers.html

www.derekburrows.com/storytelling%20tips-details.pdf

Traditional endings

www.folktale.net/endings.html

Books

Gersie, A (1997) *Reflections on therapeutic storymaking: like a piece of uncast wood* London: Jessica Kingsley

Gersie, A and King, N (1989) *Storymaking in education and therapy* London: Jessica Kingsley

Gersie, A (1991) *Earthtales: storytelling in times of change* Green Print

Grove, N (ed)(in press) *Using storytelling to support children and adults with special needs: Transforming lives through telling tales* Abingdon: Routledge

Grove, N (2005) *Ways into literature* London: David Fulton

Grove, N and Park, K (1996) *Odyssey now* London: Jessica Kingsley

Grove, N and Park, K (2000) *Developing social cognition through literature for people with learning disabilities: Macbeth in mind* London: Jessica Kingsley

Grugeon, E (1999) *The art of storytelling for teachers and pupils* London: David Fulton

Jennings, S (2004) *Creative storytelling for children at risk* London: Speechmark

Killick, S and Thomas, T (2007) *Storytelling as emotional literacy* Blackburn: Educational vPrinting Services Ltd

Mellon, N (2003) *Storytelling and the art of the imagination* Yellow Moon Press

Park, K (2004) *Interactive storytelling: developing inclusive stories for children and adults* London: Speechmark

Pellowski, A (1990) *The World of Storytelling* The H W Wilson Company

Section 9:
Appendices

Outlines example sheet

Write or draw on this page to show the important things from your story.

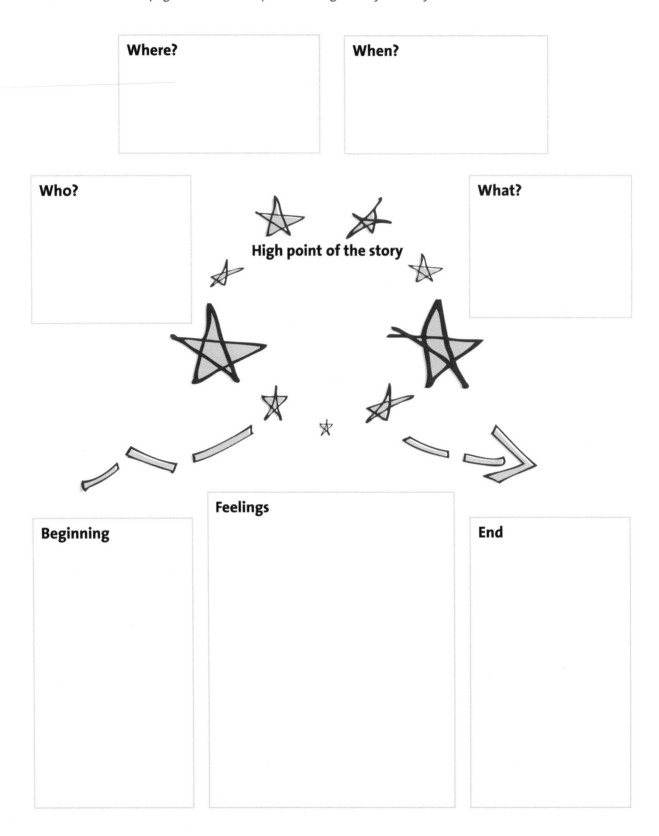

Where?

When?

Who?

What?

High point of the story

Beginning

Feelings

End

Appendix 2

Referral form

Please use this form to refer anyone whom you think would benefit from our inclusive storytelling programme or from our story activities.

Name of person: _____ Age: _____ Gender: M   F

Contact details: _____

Your name and contact details: _____

Brief description of the person and your reasons for referral: _____

Prior experience relevant to the inclusive storytelling programme
(eg any other courses and qualifications; voluntary work; arts or drama projects)

What other commitments does the person have in the week?

Strengths and needs information (please tick as appropriate)
The inclusive storytelling programme is designed for people who:

Enjoy stories	Yes	Not really	Don't know
Can use short sentences using speech, sign or communication aids	Yes	Not really	Don't know
Can follow stories and conversation	Yes	Not really	Don't know
Can remember some details of past events	Yes	Not really	Don't know
Can attend and concentrate well	Yes	Not really	Don't know
Enjoy working in groups of 10-12 people	Yes	Not really	Don't know
Are aware of the needs of others	Yes	Not really	Don't know
Can make commitments and take responsibility	Yes	Not really	Don't know

Please note:

The inclusive storytelling programme is not suitable for people who enjoy stories but:

- Prefer to work one to one or in pairs

- Need to focus on themselves before attending to the needs and interests of others

- Communicate mainly using face, vocalisations, body movement

The inclusive storytelling programme may be accessed by someone who needs support to access the experience, but this support must be provided externally.

Any health needs which should be taken into consideration at a workshop?
(eg medication and when it should be taken)

Does the person use: signing   communication aid (state what type)

Any other comments

Signed: _____   Date: _____

Thank you for completing this form. We will be in touch with you shortly

Preliminary workshop and assessment

Aims

- to give participants a feeling of the demands and opportunities of the inclusive storytelling programme

- to identify participants who would benefit from the inclusive storytelling programme, and who would do better with support activities

Story – Stone soup

This well-known tale is a good one to start with. It illustrates the principle of collaboration, how a story can be made out of almost nothing, the importance of creating expectation. It is totally non-threatening and enables everyone to join in.

A young boy is walking down the road when he sees an old man coming towards him with a pack on his back. They start to chat and the young man asks,

'Where have you come from?'

'The last village.'

'And where are you going?'

'The next village.'

'And how do you make a living if you are just travelling? Do you work?'

'Me, work, no!'

'Well how do you eat, then?'

'Just come along with me young feller me lad and I'll show you.'

So they make for the next village. In the market square the old man sets down his pack, takes out his pan, a spoon and matches and asks the boy to make a fire and bring some water from the well. The boy does so and the old chap fills his pan with water, sets it on the fire, takes a pebble from his pocket, drops it in the water and sits back.

'Whatever are you doing?' asks the boy.

'Why', says the old man 'I'm making stone soup.'

Continued

'Stone soup – what's that?'

'It's the best soup you will ever taste. Just wait and see.'

By and by and old woman wanders past. She has been to market and has a bag of onions in her hand. She stops and looks and asks,

'What are you doing?'

'I'm making stone soup.'

'Stone soup – what's that?'

'It's the best soup you will ever taste.'

'Ooh', says the old lady, 'Can I try it?'

' 'Now let me see', says the old man.'

He puts his spoon in, takes a sip, swills it round his mouth, looks up and then shakes his head.

'Well, it's good', he says, 'In fact it's very good, and it's fine for the likes of us. But for you madam – I think it needs a certain something. It's missing – now let me think – I know what it's missing! Onion. It could do with some onion.'

'Well, as it happens', says she, 'I've just bought some – you can have one to put in.'

And the old man chopped up the onion and added it to the soup and the three of them sat down and waited for it to cook.

(The story now continues with different people coming up and offering different vegetables; lastly some salt is put in. Each time there is the same dialogue, with everyone chanting the questions and answers).

And so by the end of the morning there was enough soup for all to share and they all thought it the best soup they had ever tasted. When they had all gone home, the old man washed up the pan and put it in his pack, put out the fire and said goodbye to the boy. But the stone – ah the stone. What did he do with that? Did he put it back in his pocket to take to the next village – or did he throw it in the air and leave it to fall where it landed? You decide.

Plan

Allow three hours for late arrivals and hiccups. Check referral forms to see if people need sign or communication support and make sure you can provide this.

- **Introduction and welcome to workshop**
  Health and safety information – fire exits, when breaks are happening. Explain about the inclusive storytelling programme and that this workshop is designed for both trainers and students to see if it would be a good one for them to do. Say what will happen at the end of the inclusive storytelling programme – they will get a form to take away and fill in if they would like to come (10–15 minutes).

- **Name game**
  Stand in a circle. Say your name and make a movement. Everyone copies this (10 minutes) .

- **Warm up game – Minestrone** (this links directly to the story)
  People sit in a circle. Leader goes round giving people names of vegetables. The participants swap places when their 'vegetable' names are called. When the leader shouts 'Minestrone!', everyone swaps. Note: keep names of vegetables short and limit to four at most (10–15 minutes).

- **Stone soup**
  Tell the story. Encourage people to join in (15 minutes).

- **Refreshment break**
  And informal chat (15 minutes).

- **Stone soup development**
  Who or what did the old man meet the next day? What happened? Split into two or three groups to suggest alternatives (NB have cards with possibilities for people who find it too difficult to generate ideas spontaneously). People create a picture on flip charts to share. Groups then tell their stories together (30 minutes).

- **Character game**
  Thinking of the characters we generated for the new story, group brainstorm about how each character would move, look, speak, wear (?) what they might do. Two people stand in the middle to demonstrate, others join in with what they do (10 minutes).

- **My best meal**
  In pairs, tell each other about your favourite food and the best meal you have ever eaten. The partner feeds back what the other person has told them to the main group (10 minutes: can be done in two groups each led by a trainer if necessary).

- **Feedback and what happens now.**
  Say briefly that people should let us know after the workshop if they want to come on the inclusive storytelling programme, and that we will then come and meet them with key workers to discuss it. Send ball round, everyone says what they liked, what they would change or rather do (15 minutes).

- **Closing activity**
  Take hands, move out, then all run into the centre and shout goodbye.

What to look for

Introduction game	Ability to generate an action Awareness of others Imitation ability Memory Motivation to join in group
Minestrone	Ability to co-ordinate with others Motivation to join in Attention
Stone soup story	Attention and listening Feedback responses – audience participation Enjoyment of stories
Tea break and story share	Conversational skills and relationship with others
Stone soup continued	Imagination Awareness of story conventions Ability to generate ideas Working with others – picking up and following others' ideas
Character game	Expressive ability – mime, use of face, voice and movement Imitation Awareness of others
My best meal	Language ability Descriptive skills Ability to listen and remember what others say
Feedback	Ability to reflect and contribute in group
Closing	Motivation and joining in Enjoyment Ability to leave an activity

Resources you will need

- Flip chart and plenty of large, coloured pens

- Props for the story – pan, large wooden spoon, vegetables (real or plastic) to get people going

- Tea and coffee ingredients, cups, plates, etc

Preliminary record form

Name of individual [   ]　　　　Date of workshop [   ]

Preliminary aptitude	Definintely showed this, strong candidate	Showed some skills, should be considered	Did not really show evidence of this
Motivation and interest			
Attention and listening			
Awareness of others			
Conversation skills			
Imagination and creativity			
Expressive skills in mime, voice, gesture and facial expression			
Recall of information			
Ability to reflect and contribute ideas			
Flexibility			
Imitation			

Other comments : (eg information from referral form) [   ]

Decision:

Definitely offer a place on the programme   [ ]

Consider offering a place on the course – further discussion needed   [ ]

The inclusive programme is not appropriate for this person at this time   [ ]

Signed:

Trainer

Acceptance letter

Dear (name)

Thank you for coming to our workshop.

We would like to offer you a place on the inclusive storytelling programme.

Please send us the reply slip to tell us if you are interested. Then we will arrange a preliminary interview with us and your keyworker

Yours sincerely

(name)

- -

Reply slip

☐ YES I would like to do the inclusive storytelling programme

☐ No thank you I would not like to do the inclusive storytelling programme

☐ No, I can't come on the inclusive storytelling programme now, but let me know if you are running it again

Name: Date:

Preliminary admission interview

- Tell candidates they have been successful

- Identify what impressed you about their participation in the taster workshop and what you think the inclusive storytelling programme could help them to develop

- What are their existing commitments and timetable – get them to complete a timetable. Ascertain any flexibility and fixed points

- Overview of the inclusive storytelling programme going through timetable and activities

- Contract: What is required from them:

  - Absolute commitment to doing one year of the inclusive storytelling programme, one day a week for 10-week terms

  - Leaving the inclusive storytelling programme before then depends on an interview with one of the team

  - Good time keeping (obviously taking transport into account) – getting up in time

  - Being prepared to listen and think about what they are good at, what they can change, and giving feedback to other people

  - Being prepared to try new things

  - Being prepared to work with other people and help them

  - Packed lunch needed – drinks and snacks provided

And what you will guarantee:

- Commitment to helping them learn and use their skills

- They will be in a safe confidential space

- You will liaise with key workers and families if necessary

- You will make it clear what they need to do

- You will listen to them and help them if they find things difficult

- Attending at least two storytelling sessions locally – evening or weekends. You will accompany them and make sure that transport is arranged

- Recognising achievement and progression

You need to tell them about the accreditation process. If you are not following the Open College Network accredited course, you will need to devise some other way of recognising progression.

- Do they still want to do the inclusive storytelling programme? Sign contract

If necessary, they may need to go away and consider changing their existing schedule. Need to let you know by (agreed date) if they are coming.

Information pack to send to participants at least one month prior to the start date:

- Map of centre where the inclusive storytelling sessions are taking place

- Copy of calendar and activities

- Outline of timings for a typical day – especially start, lunch and finish

- Contact details for trainers

- Transport arrangements

- Copy of any forms they have signed and their details

- Names of other students on the inclusive storytelling programme

- Photos and biographies of people teaching the inclusive storytelling programme

- Your contract with them

Contracts: Student contract

Yes, I want to do the inclusive storytelling programme *Learning to Tell*
This is what I promise to do:
- Come to every day of the inclusive storytelling programme unless I am ill
- Arrange with trainers if I have another commitment on an inclusive storytelling day
- Come to the inclusive storytelling programme on time
- Let trainers know if I cannot come
- Go to two storytelling events during the year
- Tell trainers if I do not want to go on with the inclusive storytelling programme, and have an interview with them

During the inclusive storytelling programme I will be prepared to:
- Listen and learn
- Try new things
- Say if I am not feeling OK about anything that is happening
- Work with other people in the group
- Work on my portfolio of stories
- Keep information private about other people

I understand that I need to bring with me each week:
- Packed lunch
- _____ for coffee and tea
- My portfolio
- Other things (eg hearing aid, glasses, medication)

You need to know this about me to help me learn
(Please list here any information you think would be useful)

Signed: Date:

Student:

Trainer:

Contracts: Trainer–student contract

We are really glad you are coming on the inclusive storytelling programme.
We promise you that:

- We will help you learn and use your skills

- We will provide a safe space for you to learn

- We will not tell other people information you give us that is private

- We will talk to your key workers or family if you need us to

- We will make it clear what you need to do

- We will listen to you with respect

- We will support you to visit two storytelling events

- We will tell you as soon as possible about any changes

If you want to leave the inclusive storytelling programme we will respect your wishes and give you an interview so we understand your reasons

Signed: Date:

Student:

Trainer:

Appendix 8
Student profile

Name: _____   Age: _____

Address and contact details: _____
_____

1. Your health
Please note down here anything we need to know about your health needs:

Eyesight
Do you use glasses? _____

Hearing
Do you use a hearing aid? _____

Diet _____

Medication _____

Anything else? _____

2. Communication
Please tell us anything we need to know to help you:

understand what is happening (eg signs and or pictures) _____
_____

express yourself _____
_____

If you use a communication aid, please tell us what make it is _____
_____

and who will be responsible for updating the aid with stories and new vocabulary? _____
_____

3. Reading and writing
You do not have to be able to read and write to do this course, but it is helpful for us to know about your skills.

- I can read books and newspapers
- I can read words and sentences
- I find pictures help me to understand what I read
- I need help from you to read information
- I can recognise pictures and symbols

- I can write letters and stories on my own
- I can write some words and sentences
- I can copy words and sentences

Anything else:
_____

4. Likes and dislikes

Please tell us about things that are important to you.

People:

Places:

Activities and events:

Anything else:

5. Feelings

Is there anything you find:

Funny or amusing?

Scarey or frightening?

Anything that makes you sad or angry?

Happy and calm?

Stories you like:
(Please tell us about your favourite kind of stories)

8 Life events

If appropriate, use this space to tell us about one or two events that have been important or meaningful in your life.

9 Your aims

Please tell us about things you would really like to do on the course or aims for yourself.

Timetable

Please complete this to show what you do during the week – work and leisure

Day of week	Morning	Afternoon	Evening
Monday			
Tuesday			
Wednesday			
Thursday			
Friday			
Saturday			
Sunday			

Please show us which activities you CANNOT change by putting a ✗ and which you could change if necessary with a ✓

Any other comments about your working week?

Special dates and appointments

If there are dates already arranged that cannot be changed, please list them here (eg holidays, important medical appointments).

Thank you for completing this profile. We will keep it for our records as long as you are working with us, and then we will give it back to you or destroy it.

Learning to tell